RUSSIAN FOREIGN POLICY BEYOND PUTIN

EUGENE B. RUMER

ADELPHI PAPER 390

The International Institute for Strategic Studies

Arundel House | 13–15 Arundel Street | Temple Place | London | WC2R 3DX | UK

ADELPHI PAPER 390

First published October 2007 by **Routledge**
4 Park Square, Milton Park, Abingdon, Oxon, OX14 4RN

for **The International Institute for Strategic Studies**
Arundel House, 13–15 Arundel Street, Temple Place, London, WC2R 3DX, UK
www.iiss.org

Simultaneously published in the USA and Canada by **Routledge**
270 Madison Ave., New York, NY 10016

Routledge is an imprint of Taylor & Francis, an Informa Business

DIRECTOR-GENERAL AND CHIEF EXECUTIVE John Chipman
EDITOR Patrick Cronin
MANAGER FOR EDITORIAL SERVICES Ayse Abdullah
ASSISTANT EDITOR Katharine Fletcher
PRODUCTION John Buck
COVER IMAGE Getty Images

Printed and bound in Great Britain by Bell & Bain Ltd, Thornliebank, Glasgow

British Library Cataloguing in Publication Data
A catalogue record for this book is available from the British Library

Library of Congress Cataloging in Publication Data

ISBN 978-0-415-45063-8
ISSN 0567-932X

Contents

GLOSSARY

ABM	anti-ballistic missile
BMD	ballistic missile defence
CFE	Conventional Forces in Europe
HDI	Human Development Index
LNG	liquefied natural gas
MIRVs	Multiple Independently Targeted Re-Entry Vehicles
NGOs	non-governmental organisations
SCO	Shanghai Cooperation Organisation
SRF	Strategic Rocket Forces
SSBN	ballistic missile submarine

This Adelphi Paper draws on research that the author has had the privilege of conducting over the past several years under the auspices of the Institute for National Strategic Studies, National Defense University, Washington DC. The author is grateful to the past Director of the Institute, Dr Stephen J. Flanagan, and its Director of Research and current Acting Director, Dr James A. Schear, for their support and encouragement.

Dr Patrick M. Cronin, IISS Director of Studies and Editor of the Adelphi Papers, served as a helpful guide for this project. Katharine Fletcher provided much-needed editorial expertise. Without their help this Adelphi Paper would not have been published. All remaining errors are solely the responsibility of the author.

London, August 2007

A Cool Breeze

Russia's resurgence as a strategic actor is a widely noted, but little understood feature of international relations. In Russia, it has been met with pride and satisfaction; in Europe and the United States, with barely concealed nervousness. Over the past two decades, Europe and the US have grown accustomed to the idea of Russian internal decline and retreat from the international arena. By the end of 1990s, Russia's decline and retreat were such enduring features of the international landscape that the closest observers of the country and its evolution had begun to contemplate 'a world without Russia'.[1] Behind this rather provocative phrase lay the notion that Russian weakness was reaching systemic, chronic proportions, such that Russia was becoming 'less and less an actor in world affairs, while running the risk of becoming an object of competition among more advanced and dynamic powers'.[2] This clearly is no longer the case, as Russia reasserts itself as a forceful voice on major issues of the day, from the fate of Kosovo to US missile defence in Europe.

Inside Russia, the country's economic and political stabilisation, and return to the firmament of major powers have been widely acknowledged as key accomplishments of President Vladimir Putin's term in office. Most Russian observers agree that on Putin's watch, Russia has been restored to a place in the world appropriate to its history, its stature as a nuclear superpower, its seat in all the most important councils of war and peace (the United Nations Security Council, the G8 and the NATO–Russia Council), its wealth, and the geographic expanse and unique position on the Eurasian continent that make it both a major European and Asian power.

In Europe and the United States, the Russian resurgence in the international arena has been a matter of considerable and growing discomfort partly because Russia's newly confident voice has resonated with Cold War-like echoes. These echoes, as well as stirring up troubling memories of the past, have raised new, equally troubling, concerns about the present and future.

The question of whether the West and Russia are heading into a new Cold War-style confrontation is being asked with increasing frequency on both sides of the Atlantic. Long-standing Western concerns about a Russian retreat from democracy and interference in the internal affairs of former Soviet states have been rekindled by some recent events in particular. These include Moscow's increasingly strident warnings to Europe not to cooperate with the US deployment of missile defence components to Eastern Europe; the suspension of Russia's participation in the Conventional Forces in Europe (CFE) Treaty; and the incident in May 2007 in which Estonia was subjected to virulent verbal, written and cyber attacks, apparently sponsored and coordinated by the Kremlin, in retribution for the Estonian government's decision to move the graves of Soviet soldiers from the centre of Tallinn to a less prominent position in a military cemetery.

Perhaps the most striking such recent development was the murder of renegade KGB agent Alexander Litvinenko in London in November 2006, in which another ex-KGB man was implicated in circumstances that raised questions about the Kremlin's complicity in the affair. The nature of the crime, which involved a highly controlled radioactive substance, combined with Russia's refusal to extradite the key suspect named by British authorities and its attempts to cast the Litvinenko affair as an operation sponsored by British intelligence agencies in order to discredit Russia, gave the case strong Cold War overtones, and prompted further questions about the Kremlin's intentions.

In a speech to the Munich Security Conference in February 2007, Putin declared that a new cold war could not be ruled out if the US and its NATO allies continue to meddle in Russia's internal affairs and make major decisions about international security without consulting Moscow.[3] The Russian president criticised the US for trying to create 'a world of one boss, one sovereign' and for interfering in Russian domestic politics by, for instance, presuming to tell Russia how to be democratic, while behaving itself in a most undemocratic fashion.

A few days after the speech, a senior Russian general publicly warned the governments of Poland and the Czech Republic that if they allowed US missile defence components to be deployed on their territory, they could be targeted by Russian missiles.[4] This warning, subsequently reiterated by Putin himself,[5] brought back memories of a quarter-century ago, when Soviet spokesmen made similar threats to European countries in the crisis that erupted over US plans to deploy *Pershing II* and cruise missiles in Europe in response to Soviet deployments of SS-20 missiles.

As if to underscore that his Munich speech was not an isolated episode, that Russia was not to be trifled with and that its displeasure with Western security policies was not to be dismissed, Putin delivered equally stark warnings to the West in his annual address to parliament on 27 April 2007. Once again, the Russian president sharply criticised the US and its European allies for their lack of due deference to his country's interests. Responding to the perceived challenge to Russia posed by the American missile defence deployment plans, Putin made the announcement that Russia would suspend its obligations under the CFE Treaty.[6] The treaty, signed in 1990 after more than 15 years of negotiations, had been a landmark achievement that had appeared to signal the end of East–West military confrontation. Putin could not have picked a more symbolic target for his retaliatory move.

Putin went on in May to make remarks at a ceremony commemorating Soviet victory in the Second World War that were harsher still, reminiscent of the coldest days of the Cold War, when the 'imperialist' West was painted in Soviet propaganda as the successor to Nazi Germany. The president's message effectively accused the United States of threatening Russia and the rest of the world:

> in our days such threats are not fewer. They are merely trans-
> forming, changing their appearance. And these new threats, as
> in the times of the Third Reich, [carry] the same contempt for
> human life, the same claims to global exclusivity and diktat.[7]

What next?

While Cold War echoes from Russia have certainly fuelled anxiety among Americans and Europeans about renewed East–West tensions, it is still not clear to students of Russian foreign policy and policymakers in Western capitals what drives Russian foreign policy. Is Russia, on balance, with the West or against it? What are Russia's objectives? What is the Kremlin trying to achieve in Europe? In Asia? Vis-à-vis the United States? Vis-à-vis its immediate neighbours? Finally, will Russian foreign policy change after 2008, when Putin is scheduled to leave office at the end of his second term?

The return of Russia to the firmament of major powers, and foreign policy in general, are projects to which President Putin has devoted a good deal of personal attention. Nobody has done more to determine and articulate the direction of Russian foreign policy in recent years than Putin. His active and highly visible involvement in a variety of foreign-policy activities – bilateral meetings in Russia and abroad; active participation in a variety of international fora, such as the G8, the Asia-Pacific Economic Cooperation Forum, the Association of Southeast Asian Nations regional forum and Russia–EU summits; roundtables with domestic and foreign reporters and academics, as well as general audiences; and numerous speeches dedicated to foreign affairs – leaves no room for doubt that the foreign policy of the Putin era is indeed Putin's own foreign policy. Accordingly, things could change after the president's departure.

Trying to determine who Putin's successor might be is a task that is well outside the scope of this study. This study will rather examine the underlying strategic factors that are likely to shape Russian behaviour in the international arena in the coming years, regardless of who comes to power in 2008. It seems more than likely that at least the broad outlines of Putin's foreign-policy vision will endure beyond his presidency. Putin is the first Russian leader to articulate a fully fledged foreign policy for his country after what has been a period of protracted turmoil at home and retrenchment in the international arena. Throughout his tenure, he has enjoyed the firm support of his countrymen; Putin's high approval ratings, especially in relation to his foreign policy, would suggest that his approach to international affairs has staying power. It is therefore an approach that deserves close examination.

The contention that the core elements of Putin's foreign-policy vision will endure beyond 2008 is central to this study. However, it is only one part of the argument. The other is that this vision exceeds the means that are likely to be available to the Russian government to implement it. This gap between the vision and the means, combined with changes in the international system, holds out the prospect of another readjustment of Russian foreign policy in the coming years.

Putin's foreign policy and beyond

In order to understand Putin's foreign policy, it is necessary to take a close look, not only at recent developments, but at the policies of the ten years preceding his presidency. Much of what has happened under Putin is a reaction to events in Russia's first post-Soviet decade. Following an overview of this background, this study will go on to examine the key priorities of the current approach to international relations; Putin's vision of Russian interests; and the country's view of its place in the world. The prevailing attitudes of key segments of the country's elite and general public, and the ideological landscape that lies behind current policy, will also be examined, along with the means available to Russian policymakers to advance Russian interests, and further consolidate the country's international position. The paper looks too at economic drivers, and the impact of investment flows and energy trade patterns on the country's international behaviour; also Russian perceptions of military threats, the country's capabilities to meet them, and the impact that the condition of Russia's military capability has on its posture abroad.

In conclusion, this study will address the question of how the West might deal with Russia as it re-establishes itself as a major actor in the international arena, what options Western policymakers are likely to have before them, what trade-offs they may have to contemplate, and how best they might tackle the challenges this newly confident player presents.

CHAPTER ONE

A Foreign Policy in Transition

The attention devoted by scholars and policymakers in the US and Europe at the end of Putin's second term to Russian foreign policy represents a relatively new phenomenon with respect to post-Soviet Russia. For most of the decade-and-a-half since the break-up of the Soviet Union, the attention of policy and academic communities has been drawn primarily to the country's domestic developments, and the historic changes they represented. The privatisation of the Russian economy; the introduction of competitive federal, regional and local elections; the establishment of capital markets; and reforms of currency, taxes, social welfare and various other aspects of Russia's domestic arrangements tended to monopolise the focus of Russia analysts in this period.

Active Western involvement in Russian domestic affairs in the 1990s, via advisory efforts and the delivery of various forms of economic, humanitarian and security assistance and training programmes, funded mostly by Western taxpayers, accounted for much of the interest in Russia's progress along the road to economic and political transformation in that decade. Western taxpayers and their elected representatives wanted to know that their money was being spent productively, and that as a result of that spending Russia was becoming democratic and market-oriented. Amid confusing evidence about the nature and progress of the country's domestic evolution, competing claims sparked an intense debate among academics and policy analysts about the quality of Russia's political system and economic arrangements. Was Russia a democracy? A market economy?

Were the reforms sponsored by the West helping Russia develop in the right direction? Grappling with these and other major questions, some of them unanswered to the present day, left scholars and policymakers little room to contemplate the international aspects of Russian policymaking.[1]

A 'domestic' foreign policy?

There were other reasons for the comparative neglect of foreign policy in these years. Russian foreign policy was a field in which relatively little was taking place. The country's domestic weakness and succession of political and economic crises throughout the 1990s in effect subordinated foreign affairs to domestic ones. Highly dependent on support from the United States and Europe, the Russian government did not have the luxury of pursuing a foreign-policy line substantially at odds with the policy priorities of its principal backers and donors. For most of the 1990s the country's foreign-policy agenda was dominated, to the exclusion of almost all other considerations, by relations with donors. The result was Russia's absence as an active force in international relations on many major issues.

The legacy of the final Soviet period offered few clues as to how Russia might stand on the international stage in the 1990s. The most important feature of the foreign policy of that era, under the leadership of Mikhail Gorbachev, had of course been unprecedented rapprochement with the West. Soviet withdrawal from Eastern Europe, German unification and the signing of the CFE and Intermediate-Range Nuclear Forces treaties were its major accomplishments, and they redefined the political and security landscape of Europe. As significant as they were, however, these achievements were perceived at the time in both the West and the East as repairs of damage done in the Cold War; they offered little in the way of guidance for the future. Once the repairs were completed and the Cold War decisively relegated to the past, Soviet foreign policy was left rudderless, with Soviet ideology discredited and the country's great-power ambitions having fallen prey to deteriorating material circumstances.

The question of what form its foreign policy should take remained for Russia after the Soviet Union collapsed. The domestic agenda was dominated by the multiple tasks of political and economic reforms; but how that agenda ought to manifest itself in a foreign-affairs context was not clear. How do the twin tasks of building a democratic society and a market economy translate into foreign policy?

Echoing a theme that had first emerged during the late Soviet era, the country's first post-Soviet foreign minister, Andrey Kozyrev, envisioned Russia becoming a 'normal' country. Writing in *Foreign Affairs* in early

1992, only a few months after the break-up of the Soviet Union, he stated that while Russia would not 'cease to be a great power', it would be a 'normal' great power.[2] He added that as a 'normal great power', Russia would pursue national interests that, he promised, would be 'understandable to democratic countries'.

According to Kozyrev, post-Soviet Russia would benefit from a benign international environment with few external threats. As a result, Russian foreign policy could afford to pursue goals that were dictated by the domestic agenda. He listed the following as priority steps according to that agenda: securing Russian participation in the International Monetary Fund, the World Bank and the General Agreement on Tariffs and Trade (succeeded by the World Trade Organisation in the 1990s); and establishing close relations with the G7 and the European Community (soon to become the European Union). Russia would thereby become 'a reliable partner in the community of civilized states'.[3]

Kozyrev left no doubt that foreign policy would be wholly subordinated to the task of political and economic reconstruction, which, by transforming Russia into a democracy and a market economy, would turn the country into a model citizen of the international community. In 1992, all Russian foreign policy was indeed domestic.

Many in Russia's political and foreign policy elite rejected Kozyrev's agenda at the time, and its impact on Russian foreign policy in the 1990s may well have been exaggerated. But his vision is important to note nevertheless, because it is still remembered in Russia as a symptom of the country's decline and retreat during that decade. Kozyrev remains significant, if only as a symbol of what many Russians do not want to revisit.

Post-Cold War context

Kozyrev's approach to the new country's foreign policy was not unique in the early part of the post-Cold War era. In fact, it mirrored – and quite likely was influenced by – the prevailing thinking about foreign policy and international relations in policy and academic communities in the West during that time.

Global, democratic, market-oriented

At the end of the Cold War, the victory of the liberal democratic idea was beyond dispute. The great ideological stand-off between liberal democracy and communism was over; communism had suffered a defeat of historic proportions that had put an end to it as a political ideology. The reach of liberal democracy could only increase. The prevailing view was that liberal democracy held the answer to the challenge of instability and was the only form of political organisation capable of ensuring long-term stability.

Just as liberal democracy triumphed over communism, market capitalism proved victorious over central planning. It was the only form of economic organisation that could secure the fundamental conditions for healthy economic development, as well as the necessary conditions for liberal democracies to prosper. This was held to have been borne out with particular clarity in the former Soviet bloc; the site of the dramatic downfall of communism and central planning.

The importance of free markets was underscored by the new phenomenon of globalisation. The triumph of market capitalism coincided with a period of rapid technological change. Together, the freedom of ideas and the freedom of markets would make it possible for new technologies to spread rapidly and introduce a new era in which the world would become more interconnected and prosperous than ever before. People, ideas, goods, capital and technology would flow across political and geographical boundaries freely and rapidly. Those interfering with the free flow or not ready to join the global express would pay a heavy price, because the 'invisible hand' of the free market was never mistaken.

The spread of liberal democracy would, the thinking went, produce greater accountability on the part of governments, whose policies would also be judged by markets, which would react swiftly to bad decisions, prompting an equally swift response on the part of the electorate. Thus, good policies would be adopted in the self-interest of governments. The long-term – or sustainable, to use the term that came into fashion at the time – stability and prosperity of a given nation thus hinged on its ability and commitment to establish free markets and democratic governance, in line with the rules of the globalising world, as made by the free market.[4] In this atmosphere, one might begin to wonder whether a nation needed a foreign policy at all.[5]

Betting on transition

The 'transition paradigm',[6] embraced by many in academic and policy circles in the 1990s, was an elaboration of elements of this vision. In this view, the world was witnessing an unstoppable progression towards democracy, which would eventually become, in effect, the universal form of governance.

Very broadly, all countries could be divided into three categories: those that were democracies; those that were not; and those that were in transition from the latter to the former. The choice before the last, transitioning, group was either to succeed and join the democratic camp, or else fail and either fail as a state, as in the case of Afghanistan or Haiti, or join the pariahs, such as North Korea and Iraq.

Since, it was also held, democracies don't wage wars on one another, this wave of democratisation would bring with it unprecedented harmony in international relations. With major war relegated to history with the end of the Cold War, the only conflict the international community would now face would be between democracies and non-democracies. As for the countries in transition, they might face some frictions along the way, but as they made progress and integrated in the community of democratic nations, they too would relegate armed conflict to their pasts. Such conflicts as emerged from the ruins of the old international order – in Nagorno-Karabakh, in the Balkans – were both the final gasps of the old and the birth pangs of the new international order.

In short, though not an outright repudiation of balance-of-power theory, much of the prevalent thinking about international relations shortly after the end of the Cold War at least posited an unprecedented fusion of inter-ests and values across states. In the global marketplace of ideas and goods, the balance of power and interests would be decided by the market's invis-ible hand.

This was the intellectual context in which Russia inaugurated its new foreign policy in the early 1990s. Foreign Minister Kozyrev's policy, as articulated in his 1992 *Foreign Affairs* article, fitted the mood of the moment perfectly. It made sense that Russia would in effect need no 'foreign policy' as such, that its position in the international community would be deter-mined by its domestic condition.

It should also be noted that Russian preoccupation with domestic affairs suited Western interests in any case. The United States and its NATO allies were free to pursue their foreign-policy objectives (for such things, the new international order notwithstanding, did still exist) without needing to worry about accommodating Moscow's concerns, mollifying the Russians or countering Russian actions. 'A world without Russia' was quite conve-nient for the US and its allies.

Russia in this period was the pre-eminent example of a country in tran-sition. Its transition was taking place on such a scale and was of such scope that, if successful, it would revolutionise the international system. It was clear that a transition of such magnitude could not be a discrete event, would involve steps backward as well as forward, be difficult to measure and would take a long time to complete. Policymakers on both sides of the

Atlantic spoke about it in terms of vast generational change that would take decades to accomplish. They counselled patience – strategic patience – when dealing with Russia. They reassured themselves and their Western publics that things would only improve with time. As older generations who resisted progress moved on, younger ones would take their place, and the forces of progress would eventually prevail.[7]

Western policies towards Russia were built on the assumption that, at the end of this transition, Russia would indeed become a democracy, a 'normal' country, a pillar of the Euro-Atlantic security structure. Alternatives were not much discussed, nor were the roots of any other outcome very apparent. A return to the country's totalitarian past did not bear thinking about. The other possibility – further disintegration of the Russian state, culminating in state failure – was also too much to contemplate publicly in the context of a country with thousands of nuclear weapons. There appeared to be simply no alternative to the transition's success.

In the meantime, however, the transition paradigm, perhaps unsurprisingly, offered little guidance with respect to the foreign policy of a country in transition, and events in Europe and elsewhere in the world would not wait for Russia to emerge from its transformation with a new domestic arrangement and a foreign policy to match. Those events had to be responded to, with or without Russia. The US and its European allies, acting as the principal architects of the new post-Cold War international order, proceeded on the basis of their assumptions about Russia and the eventual results of its transition.

In practical terms this meant expanding NATO into Eastern Europe; intervening militarily in the Balkans to put an end to inter-ethnic bloodshed; actively engaging Moscow's former satellites in the former Soviet Union in security cooperation programmes; and promoting energy export schemes from former Soviet countries, bypassing Russia. More often than not the Russian government objected to these moves, but, necessarily focused on its domestic challenges, it was rarely, if ever, in a position to do much about them.

Western policy was not, however, confined to simply ignoring Russia. Confident that Russia's transformation would be successful, and interpreting Russian opposition to many of the West's policies as a short-term phenomenon, Europe and the United States took Russian leaders at their word when they said that they aspired to turn their country into a 'normal' member of the community of democratic nations at peace with themselves and each other, and actively sought to engage Russia in a broad effort 'to build Europe whole and free'.[8]

This policy manifested itself in Russia's participation in the G7 summits and its formal admittance to the group in 1997; efforts by NATO to engage Russia in a dialogue and a broad security cooperation agenda; and Russian involvement in peacekeeping operations in the Balkans. Europe and the United States believed that by giving Russia a place at the table, they could reinforce a Russian commitment to pursuing a new, 'normal' foreign policy, and help to give that foreign policy the right shape.

A less frequently articulated aspect of Western policy towards Russia was that aspects of it would provide a hedge against the unconscionable alternative of Russia failing in its transition and re-emerging as a threat to Europe, as either a totalitarian or a failing state. By expanding NATO and securing Russia's periphery, the thinking was at the time, the West would put itself in a better position to cope with that kind of Russia.[9]

For much of the past 15 years, this approach seemed to have worked well, from the Western point of view. NATO has expanded twice and now includes all Moscow's former Warsaw Pact allies and three Baltic states, all of which are also members of the European Union. The Balkans are at peace, with a settlement for Kosovo in the works. The US and its European allies are actively engaged in the search for security and stability in Ukraine, the Caucasus and Central Asia. Russia and NATO have established a forum for consultations and are engaged in discussions about joint missile defence projects for Russia and Europe, among other things. Following its withdrawal from the Cold War Anti-Ballistic Missile (ABM) Treaty in 2002, the US signed a new agreement with Russia – the 'Moscow Treaty' – to drastically reduce the two countries' strategic nuclear arsenals, thus inaugurating a new arms-control regime and strategic nuclear relationship between the two former adversaries. All these are elements of a transatlantic post-Cold War architecture that includes Russia and its former satellites, and that is premised on a shared vision of Europe 'whole and free', with Russia as one of its central pillars.[10]

But this array of accomplishments, though impressive, tells only one part of the story of relations between Russia and the West since the early 1990s. The story also includes the strikingly steadfast Russian opposition over the course of 15 years to much in the West's foreign policy, including several of the achievements listed, notably the eastward expansion of NATO; NATO's military actions in the Balkans, which flared up in the crisis at the Pristina airport in Kosovo in 1999, during which Russian and NATO troops stood on the brink of a military confrontation; the US unilateral withdrawal from the ABM Treaty; the new, flexible US approach to strategic arms control as laid out in the Moscow Treaty; US and NATO involvement in the countries of the former Soviet Union; and the planned deployment of American ballistic missile defence (BMD) components to the Czech Republic and Poland.

Though specific disputes have been resolved without apparent long-term consequences, in retrospect this part of the story raises major questions with respect to both the extent and quality of the Russian commitment to the foreign-policy course that was outlined by Kozyrev in 1992, and the West's understanding of Russia over this period.

For most of the post-Cold War era, such Russian positions as opposition to NATO's eastward expansion or to Western involvement in the former Soviet states were considered by the West to be part of the Soviet legacy, hanging over Russian foreign policy attitudes as the country struggled with the challenge of transition. Despite virtually universal opposition to NATO's extension into Eastern Europe from Russians of all political persuasions, from reformers to reactionaries, the prevailing attitude among Western policymakers was that Russia would eventually have no choice but to accept the expansion; once Russia recovered from its troubles and joined the community of market democracies, it would develop a new appreciation for the peace and stability that Western institutions brought to its otherwise turbulent borderlands.[11]

Beyond transition

In 2007, key indicators of Russia's domestic condition suggest that Russia has emerged from transition, sooner than many had projected it would. Its economy has experienced strong growth for nearly a decade. The rouble is stable, foreign currency reserves have surpassed the $400 billion mark, and foreign investment is booming.[12] The endless succession of political crises that plagued the country throughout the 1990s is now in the past. Russia has a youthful and dynamic leader who is focused, dedicated to consolidating Russia's recovery as a great power, and who enjoys a level of personal popularity among his citizens that makes him the envy of most other leaders on either side of the Atlantic. Furthermore, he appears determined to observe the constitution and step down from the presidency at the end of his second term – a milestone that, if achieved, will mark a new measure of political maturity for Russia.

Russia has shown a confident posture in the international arena, consolidating its relationship with China, appearing to expand its influence in the former Soviet states and playing a role in several major international developments – vis-à-vis Iran, North Korea and the Kosovo settlement. Russian representatives, beginning with President Putin, have been speaking in increasingly self-assured tones, declaring their intention that Russia should play the role of active participant in the international system, be a leader, not a joiner, a major power no longer content to live in a unipolar world with the United States at its centre.[13] In both domestic and foreign spheres, the evidence points to a country that has put its years of decline and searching behind it and has confidently, and at times stridently, started anew.

Had the initial assumptions of the post-Cold War era been correct, a confident post-transition Russia would have emerged from its internal transformation as a key participant in the NATO-based European security architecture; specifically, working with other European nations and the US to secure a lasting solution for Kosovo; decisively imposing sanctions on Iran; and welcoming the plans for US BMD components in Poland and the Czech Republic as complementary to its own discussions of European missile defence cooperation with NATO.

Needless to say, it has not; Russia's activity on these issues has not been of the kind that the West might have hoped for, indeed, each of them has emerged as a point of serious disagreement between Russia and the transatlantic alliance. Although none appears to be sufficiently weighty in its own right to alter radically the relationship between Russia and the West, when taken together, these, along with several other contentious issues, such as the quality of Russian democracy and the Russian use of the energy trade for strategic advantage, have contributed to the creation of a real diplomatic gap between East and West; a sharp contrast to the situation only a few years ago, when much talk was of 'partnership'.

A detailed discussion of whether or not the Russian transition is truly over, where the country is at this moment in its political development, and where it is heading, lies well outside the scope of this study. For the purposes of this discussion, the key point is that Russian foreign policy today does not conform to the expectations that were prevalent in Russia, as well as in the West, in the early years after the end of the Cold War. It is not the foreign policy of a country that is content to be 'normal' like any other in the community of market democracies.

CHAPTER TWO

Putin's Foreign Policy – A Matter of Interest

The foreign policy that is emerging towards the end of President Putin's second term displays, in striking contrast to the Kozyrev agenda of 1992, a number of unmistakable realpolitik qualities. The Putin era has seen the development of an international posture primarily focused on interests and the balance of power. Putin himself has adumbrated this approach as being the typical basis for international relations:

> Interest has been the main principle in the international arena and in relations between states throughout history. But as these relations became more civilised, it became more and more clear that one's own interests should be compared with the interests of other countries.[1]

While the Kozyrev blueprint recommended Russian integration into the ranks of other nations guided by shared principles and ideals, Putin's approach posits Russia as a major power, one of a handful of gravitational poles in the international system that determine its shape and direction.

Integration has not been abandoned by Russia under Putin; it remains an important objective in Russian foreign policy. Russia has not and will not become a hermit kingdom. But the kind of integration it pursues is of a different kind to that of Kozyrev's vision, in which integration was into an international system that was essentially based on common values. It is instead founded on a vision of international relations in which values and principles play a minor role, if any at all, and the course of history is determined by the balance of power and interests among countries, major powers in particular.

A major power

The theme of Russia as a gravitational pole in world affairs, a full member of the community of major powers, a voice to be heard and a presence to be reckoned with, permeates Putin's foreign-policy statements.

Russia's international resurgence has been made possible by its domestic revival. Among other rewards, economic growth has enabled Russia to repay its international debts, which Putin has referred to as 'catastrophic', and the country's combined gold and foreign currency reserves now rank third in the world.[2] These reserves provide the country with the cushion and flexibility to pursue ambitious domestic and foreign policies.

Equally, success abroad feeds progress at home: as Putin observed in a speech to senior Russian diplomats in June 2006, 'countries' international activities constitute an increasingly important component of national development'.[3] The counsel of the Putin years, therefore, is that Russia should not be content to be a passive member of the community of nations, accepting the guidance of others, for other powers have their own interests, and little regard for the interests of others. Rather, Russia should preserve and build on its successes by actively participating in formulating the global agenda. Only then, Putin has said, will Russian interests be adequately protected and advanced, balance be maintained in international relations, and dangerous trends, for example the proliferation of weapons and related technologies, be checked.[4] Putin's emphasis on the symbiosis between domestic affairs and Russia's international standing curiously mirrors Kozyrev's, whose very different vision also stressed the indivisibility of Russia's domestic and foreign-policy agendas.

Few inside or outside Russia will be able to avoid making favourable comparisons between the legacy Putin will leave to his successor and the balance sheet he inherited from Boris Yeltsin. Crippled by domestic decline and burdened by foreign debt, Yeltsin's Russia could at best limp along in the international arena; Putin's Russia, unencumbered by debt or dependency on foreign lenders, appears well positioned to act as an independent power. Putin has therefore made clear that Russia has no intention of joining anybody else's 'holy alliances';[5] that it is willing to cooperate and conduct dialogue *as an equal*; and that, while it does not seek confrontation, it will make sure to promote and defend its interests.[6]

A sphere of influence

Of those interests, none has been articulated more frequently, clearly, or with greater consistency throughout the post-Soviet period than the consolidation of a Russian sphere of influence among the former countries of the Soviet Union.[7] Establishing Russian pre-eminence throughout the former Soviet Union is central to Russia's political, security and economic interests:

a) Political and security interests

Politically, securing Russia's position as the epicentre of power and influence in the post-Soviet space would communicate prestige and confirm Russia as a great power and a pole of the multipolar world. As Russian analyst of international affairs Dmitri Trenin has noted, 'No great power … walks alone':[8] close allies, even satellite nations, are a crucial part of a major power's armoury.

The geopolitical, balance-of-power frame of mind that has dominated recent Russian thinking in international relations is also concurrent with the idea that Russian security interests call for Moscow to maintain a security belt around its periphery, made up of satellites compliant with Russian policy preferences. Most of Russia's neighbours are seen by Moscow as not stable or strong enough to maintain independent foreign and security policies adequate to protect Russian security interests. If left to their own devices, Moscow believes, these states will end up in a security vacuum. They may find themselves falling prey to general instability, aggravated by various uncontrolled dark elements of globalisation such as transnational crime, terrorism and inter-ethnic, inter-confessional militancy, thus potentially posing an even greater threat to Russian security. Alternatively, they might be pulled into the orbits of other major powers, which, in the balance-of-power framework, would not serve Russian interests well.

Active Russian opposition to the popular pro-democracy movements, or 'colour revolutions', in neighbouring Georgia in 2003 and Ukraine in 2004 attracted considerable attention in the West, and contributed to increased East–West tensions. Few, if any, Russian policy analysts, let alone officials, appear to believe in the genuinely democratic quality of these popular movements. They maintain that they are essentially chaotic, and dangerous, and that, if left unchecked, movements like these could lead to instability on Russia's doorstep, and so therefore must be opposed. Western support for the colour revolutions is seen as naive and misguided at best, and deliberately hostile to Russian interests at worst, intended to further isolate and encircle Russia and deny it any influence it still has in an area where Russia's interests are far greater than those of the West.

b) Military interests

Russia's opposition to US plans to deploy BMD components in Poland and the Czech Republic is the subject of serious controversy.[9] The most widely cited reason for this opposition is the unilateral nature of US plans and the lack of consultations with Russia, which the Kremlin sees as a challenge to its standing as a great power.[10] Any direct military threat posed by the deployments has been largely discounted, though some Russian and foreign analysts have pointed out that under certain circumstances US interceptors could interdict Russian missiles during the early, boost phase. The deployments represent a problem for Russian military planners largely because of this possibility, and the challenge it could present to Russia's strategic parity with the United States.[11] Russian planners are also likely to be concerned that bases that currently have limited capabilities could be augmented.

In the conventional military sphere, the need for a security belt around Russia is a major preoccupation. To the current generation of Russian military leaders, whose formative years coincided with some of the tensest periods of the Cold War and the military stand-off in Europe, the modern-day 'correlation of forces' does not bode well. The Baltic nations are members of NATO, the Alliance conducts exercises on Ukrainian territory, and Moscow is well within the range of US precision-guided weapons combined with enhanced reconnaissance capabilities, or 'reconnaissance-strike complexes', to use a term borrowed from former Soviet Chief of the General Staff Marshal Nikolay Ogarkov, who forecast in the early 1980s the advent of long-range precision-guided munitions and their impact on warfare.[12]

c) Economic interests

Russia's military–strategic interests go hand-in-hand with its economic interests. Energy exports to Europe are the cornerstone of Russia's economic wellbeing, as well its trump card in relation to the other major powers. Exports have to traverse the post-Soviet and former Warsaw Pact states in order to reach the most lucrative European markets. From Moscow's point of view, its lack of control over pipelines to key markets constitutes a critical Russian vulnerability.[13] Friendly, compliant governments in the countries on its periphery would boost Russia's security, economic security and strategic leverage vis-à-vis Europe.

Russia has other, long-standing, economic interests with its neighbours. Trade and labour migration patterns and transport infrastructure show that Russia and its neighbours are still mutually dependent, having shared an economic system for decades. Protecting this economic sphere of influence is an important interest, especially in Russia's current mercantilist, geopolitical frame of mind.

Limited influence

Though Russia continues to matter a great deal to the countries on its periphery, it is no longer the all-powerful actor in the neighbourhood. Over the years, Moscow has attempted to assemble various regional umbrella organisations and placed itself at their apex in order to consolidate its hold over the region, including the Collective Security Treaty Organisation and the Eurasian Economic Community. None appears to be functioning as a conduit of Russian influence, or indeed functioning much at all.

Russia's heavy-handedness undercuts its influence with its neighbours and spurs them to seek closer relations with the West. Aggressive Russian 'energy diplomacy' toward Georgia, Armenia, Azerbaijan, Moldova and Ukraine, for instance, has given an added momentum to these countries' already active interest in forging closer relations with NATO, the EU and the US.

A preference among ex-Soviet states for looking to the West and elsewhere on issues of energy trade was illustrated, somewhat startlingly for Russia, in the aftermath of recent negotiations between Russia and Central Asian states. President Putin invested a great deal of time and personal prestige in the task of securing a pledge from Central Asian leaders to sell more of their gas to Russia. His success in this project, following a trip to Central Asia in May 2007,[14] was announced with much fanfare as a gain for Russian interests and a blow to competing Western energy schemes. However, not long after Putin's trip, the leaders of Kazakhstan and Turkmenistan made it clear that their agreements with Putin were not the last word in their energy export plans, and that they planned to look for other export markets and outlets besides Russia.[15]

The waning influence of Russia in its own neighbourhood may be summed up in the words of a study by the Council for Foreign and Defence Policy, the leading Russian think tank for national security and foreign policy, which described the very idea of a post-Soviet space as a 'disappearing reality'.[16] The authors of the study predict that different parts of the region will increasingly feel the gravitational pull of other centres of power – chiefly China and Europe – leading to its eventual disintegration as a political unit of any meaningful kind. According to the report, Russia will continue to have a major stake in countries around its periphery, but its ability to pursue its interests there will be constrained by the diminishing resources available to it and stiffer competition from other power centres.[17]

In the future, the success or failure of Russia's policy towards its neighbours will be determined by its ability to be an attractive centre of gravity of its own, capable of countering the political and economic pull from the West and the East, and its ability to act as a security provider to regional states. In view of its recent record, Russia's prospects in this sphere look mixed at best.

Beyond the sphere of influence: the Middle East and the world of Islam

While not as important to it as its closest neighbours, the Middle East is nevertheless an area of concern to Russian policymakers, largely because of its proximity to Russia's turbulent southern borders. Russia's influence in the Middle East is nowhere near as great as that enjoyed by the Soviet Union. Absent the resources – economic, military and political – necessary to sustain Soviet-era relationships and counter US and European influence, Russian diplomacy has been limited to taking a handful of niche opportunities. This has included making overtures to Iran, Syria and Hamas, all of which have welcomed the opportunity to break out of their international isolation, but which have done little to enhance Moscow's influence in the Middle East and political capital elsewhere. Russia's moves towards these actors have undermined its position in the coalition of major powers seeking to promote Middle East peace.[18]

Gestures towards Hamas and relations with Iran have also done little to make up for the long shadow cast over Russia's reputation in the Islamic world by the war in Chechnya. Russia's recognition of Israel and its expressions of support for the global 'war on terror', widely perceived as a US-led war on Islam, also undermine its position in the Islamic world.

Relations with the Islamic world are important to Russia, and represent a major challenge for its foreign policy. Russia has its own sizeable Muslim minority, estimated at 13% of its total population.[19] Russian Muslims are no longer isolated from their co-religionists abroad, as they were during the Soviet era, and, as the unstable situation in the North Caucasus where many of this population lives would suggest, they have experienced radicalisation much like the rest of the Muslim world.

Although Russia has important economic concerns in the Middle East (energy and arms trade are at the top of the list), its main concern there is likely therefore to remain security. The region's further destabilisation is something that most Russian analysts view as potentially posing a direct threat to Russian security. Russian policy has thus been aimed at minimising that volatility and avoiding such destabilisation. This policy has entailed opposition to the war in Iraq, as a cause of greater regional instability; obtaining membership in the Organisation of Islamic Countries in order to project the image of Russia as a friend of Islam; maintaining the relationship with Iran; courting Hamas in an effort to win grassroots support among Muslims; and other steps intended to position Russia in Middle Eastern minds as occupying a different place in the international arena from a West seen as inherently hostile to Islam.[20]

As we have seen, the successes of this policy have so far been limited. It remains to be seen how effective an approach it will prove to be in the long run. Unlike US policy in the Middle East, which has sought to bring about long-term, systemic change in the region, Russian policy has been aimed at preserving the status quo and avoiding major changes. As the region changes nevertheless, this policy may well prove no more successful than US attempts to pre-empt change. All the same, Russian policymakers show few signs of modifying their tendency to deal with challenges from the Middle East largely on the hoof; confining diplomacy to making concilia-tory noises as and when necessary to restore a fragile balance.

Russian interests and other major powers

Russia's relations with the other major powers – the United States, Europe and China – defy easy characterisation. Beyond Russia's desire for recog-nition and treatment as a major presence in the international arena, its interests amount to a mix of near-term factors and long-term considerations that reflect many of the uncertainties facing Russia abroad and at home.

The United States and Europe – rivals, partners
Currently, Russian relations with Europe and the US are dominated by Russia's pursuit of its special sphere of influence in the former Soviet lands, and by debates about the future of Kosovo and related post-Cold War settlements, energy trade and BMD.

I: Russia's front yard, Europe's backyard

The membership of all of Moscow's former Warsaw Pact and Baltic satellites in NATO and the European Union has fundamentally altered the political geography of Europe and the dynamics of Russia–EU relations. What was once Eastern Europe, Moscow's extended security belt, the Warsaw Pact and the Council for Mutual Economic Assistance, is now Central Europe, NATO's 'in area', and the EU. Countries that Russia considers to be in its front yard and would like to see solidly in its sphere of influence – Ukraine, Belarus, Moldova, Georgia – are now in the EU's backyard. Most are eager participants in a wide variety of NATO-sponsored activities designed to expand the Euro-Atlantic security architecture. Some have openly embraced the goal of joining the EU and NATO. Together they make up a region in which the EU is busy formulating its interests and promoting its policies.

This rapprochement – in the most literal sense – between Russia's front yard and the EU's backyard has created ample opportunities for tensions. The EU's emphasis on the promotion of democratic governance and the rule of law has come into direct conflict with the Russian emphasis on defending interests and the balance of power; for example during the 'colour revolutions', and in the EU's dealings with Belarus. The American embrace of democracy promotion as a major instrument and objective of its foreign policy also pitted the US against Russia over the colour revolutions. Maintaining Russian influence in this contested region, shielding the region from destabilising Western democracy-promotion schemes and keeping more countries in the region from joining NATO are what Moscow sees as the key requirements for security and stability on its doorstep, and priorities in its relationship with both Washington and Brussels.

II: Kosovo and other regional conflicts

One issue that has emerged as a source of considerable disagreement between Russia, on the one hand, and the US and Europe, on the other, is Kosovo. Despite Kosovo being outside the former Warsaw Pact and the Soviet Union, events there are nevertheless likely to reverberate throughout the former Eastern bloc lands, where several conflicts are 'frozen', awaiting resolution. Europe and the US have accepted the notion of Kosovo's independence from Serbia, indeed they have advocated it as the solution to the 'last substantial territorial issue remaining from the violent collapse of Yugoslavia'.[21] Russia has opposed it on the grounds that it would set a dangerous precedent for other potential and actual breakaway territories;[22] that the partition of a sovereign state against its will is wrong; and that the recognition of Kosovan independence alongside the rejection of similar aspirations on the part of Russian-backed Abkhazia and South Ossetia shows a double standard. The preferred Russian solution to the tensions in Kosovo is further talks between Serbia and Kosovo until a mutually acceptable solution is found.[23]

Russia's opposition to the Kosovo independence plan runs deep. Russian interests would be best served by freezing the Kosovo situation, and indeed any other post-Cold War conflict or conflict aftermath, indefinitely. This is because, for the time being at least, Russian interests will be adversely affected no matter how such conflicts are resolved. Were the US and Europe to agree on the precedent-setting nature of the proposed Kosovo settlement, Russia would be compelled to confront the prospect of Chechnya, or any other independence-minded constituency, taking advantage of it.[24] The Kremlin would then run the risk of seeing its influence diminish throughout its region, as its client states and regimes emerged from their post-Soviet isolation and pursued recognition and economic opportunities in Europe, most likely at the expense of their ties to Russia. Thus, for the foreseeable future, Russian interests are best served by the status quo.

The proposed settlement also serves as an embarrassing reminder to Russian elites of the days when, as most Russian foreign-policy analysts believe was the case, the US and Europe imposed their own unilateral solution on the Balkans without consulting Russia. The Yeltsin government, in this view, was too weak and too corrupt to stand up to the West. Now, it is felt, the Russians must not allow what in their view was an illegitimate decision to become the legitimate expression of the will of the international community.

III: A matter of energy

An equally important set of Russian interests is at stake with regard to energy trade and security. Russia's oil and gas exports have been at the heart of the country's economic revival, and the country's proud claim to the status of 'energy superpower' hinges on its ability to supply and transport energy to key customers, Europe in particular. Increasingly, though, there is a feeling of urgency around securing this pre-eminence: Russia is experiencing a shortfall in its gas production, and forecasts indicate that it is likely to have increasing difficulty meeting both its export obligations and domestic consumption requirements in the future.[25]

Russian officials and energy companies view Central Asian gas reserves as the critical hedge against this decline in domestic production. Russia's current near-monopoly on access to Central Asian exports also gives it strategic leverage with supplier nations in Central Asia, as well as the European consumers downstream. Putin's intensive – and ultimately unsuccessful – diplomacy in Central Asia in May 2007 is a recent signal of Russia's interest in locking in its access to this energy source.

But Europe's pursuit of the diversification of its energy supply has in recent years prompted it to devise schemes for the construction of a gas pipeline connecting consumers in Eastern, Central and Western Europe with Central Asian suppliers, bypassing Russia. Such schemes not only threaten to undercut Russia's strategic position in the former Soviet lands and dilute its influence vis-à-vis Europe, but cut into its gas imports for domestic use and endanger the country's economic wellbeing. US active support and encouragement of such schemes heightens Russian concerns about its core interests. Preventing the construction of pipelines to Europe outside its own territory therefore constitutes an important Russian objective in its relations with Europe and the United States.

IV: The BMD problem

The prominence of the missile defence issue on the bilateral US–Russian agenda warrants further analysis of this theme. In Russian eyes, in contrast to issues such as the place of Russia's former Soviet allies in the international arena, the US's capability to deploy a variety of military assets on the territory of these states, and the energy trade, which clearly directly affect a broader range of countries and interests, the issue of US BMD in Europe has a distinctly bilateral quality. Against American objections that US missile defence deployment in, say, Poland, is a matter for the US and Poland alone, Russian policymakers maintain that, on the contrary, the implications of US actions in this area are profound for Russia in particular, because of the presumed potential impact on the US–Russian strategic nuclear balance. In the long run, from the standpoint of Russian strategic planners, no point of contention between the US and Russia is likely to be more important to the relationship between the two countries.

Ever since the US withdrawal from the ABM Treaty, many in Russia have worried that US BMD programmes are now largely unconstrained, and there is a widespread belief in the country that, in the military sphere, Russia is no match for the United States. These concerns are likely to be feeding Russian perceptions that US BMD could in the future pose a meaningful challenge to the Russian nuclear deterrent, especially once Russia has further reduced its number of missiles, as planned in line with the Moscow Treaty.[26] Assurances from the United States that it has no intention of undermining Russian strategic nuclear deterrent capabilities have so far fallen on deaf ears. Few in Moscow's national security community take such assurances at face value, on the grounds that the West has given Russia strategic assurances before and broken them when its interests so required, as in the case of the expansion of NATO.[27]

Russian concerns on this matter were further provoked in 2006 by the publication in *Foreign Affairs* of an article by two US academics arguing that the world was entering the era of US nuclear primacy.[28] The article elicited angry protests from Russian commentators, some of whom even perceived it as an attempt by the US to engage in 'psychological warfare' with Russia.[29]

This neuralgic response to the idea that strategic parity with the United States might be slipping away illustrates the importance of this issue to Russia and its foreign-policy elite. The end of strategic parity would, in Russian eyes, jeopardise Russia's great-power aspirations and undermine the country's standing in the world, thus diminishing its leverage with the other major powers. Fundamentally, Russian policymakers and analysts have long argued that in the absence of a robust conventional capability, the country's strategic nuclear forces remain the guarantor of its independence, sovereignty and security.[30] Russia's nuclear arsenal ensures that it can pursue its interests in the international arena without the threat of nuclear blackmail.[31] Without a reliable nuclear deterrent, Russia would once again lose its sovereignty and become a pawn of other powers, as it was in the 1990s. Thus, to the extent that US plans for missile defence pose even the most remote challenge to the country's nuclear deterrent, Russian interests demand that no effort is spared in stopping them.

V: Coincidence of interests

Not all Russian interests in relation to Europe and the US call for competition with these powers. In a number of areas American, European and Russian interests coincide; in some other areas they do not necessarily coincide, but there nevertheless exist concerns that act as constraints on the powers' willingness and ability to compete.

Such areas include post-Soviet Central Asia and Afghanistan, Iran, counter-terrorism and counter-narcotics. Although Russian policy and rhetoric have at times prompted doubts among policymakers and Russia-watchers as to whether Russia does indeed have interests in common with the West in these areas, on balance they do appear to be areas where at least some intersection of interests can be found.

a) Central Asia

Along Russia's periphery, Central Asia stands out as a region in which Russian interests have on various occasions coincided with those of the

US and Europe, and on others dramatically diverged. Since the break-up of the Soviet Union, the region, which includes five former Soviet republics (Kazakhstan, Uzbekistan, Kyrgyzstan, Tajikistan and Turkmenistan) has been the scene of both cooperation and competition between the US and its allies and Russia. The most important geopolitical developments in Central Asia in this period have been the emergence of US and European policies to build multiple pipelines to link the energy-rich Caspian states to Western markets, bypassing Russia; the rise of the Taliban in Afghanistan (which borders Uzbekistan, Turkmenistan and Tajikistan); and the growing presence of China in the region.

The first has, as we have seen, been a source of contention between the Russia and the Western powers. Russian concerns about European pipeline plans detailed above are particularly acute in view of the success of an earlier, similar, American scheme to build an oil pipeline from the Caspian to the Mediterranean, bypassing Russia. A key objective of US policy in the 1990s was to provide Caspian oil and gas producers an outlet to world markets bypassing Russia, to enhance their independence and reduce the Russian hold on their exports. That policy resulted in the construction of the Baku–Tbilisi–Ceyhan oil pipeline, which was completed in 2005.

The struggle between Russia, seeking to retain its position in Central Asia, and the US and Europe, intent on opening Central Asia to multiple markets and preventing a Russian monopoly on Central Asian gas exports, has intensified in recent years with the European pipeline schemes discussed above. The rise in energy prices worldwide promises to make the competition for control of energy transportation in the region all the more vigorous yet.

The second development, the rise of the Taliban in Afghanistan, became an area of shared concern among the US, Europe, Russia and the Central Asian countries themselves in the late 1990s. The radical regime was viewed by all as a threat to regional stability and as offering terrorists a safe haven. The commonality of US–Russian–Central Asian interests vis-à-vis the Taliban manifested itself most vividly in the aftermath of the 11 September 2001 attacks, when Central Asian states opened their doors to the US and European military presence in support of the war in Afghanistan, and Russia endorsed the war and offered its support and cooperation.

However, the US presence in Central Asia has been a source of some unease in Russia and a great deal of ambivalence among Russian policymakers since the beginning, very soon after 11 September.[32] A US and NATO military presence in Russia's backyard was seen as potentially posing a threat to Russian influence in the former Soviet countries. Equally, however, Russia had a compelling interest in seeing the Taliban defeated, as that rogue regime posed a threat to Russia's neighbours and to its own heartland.[33]

These competing interests have resulted in a changeable Russian approach. Having accepted the US and NATO presence in Central Asia in 2001, Russia then opened an air base in Kant, Kyrgyzstan, in what was a fairly transparent attempt to show its flag and counter the American presence at the nearby base at Manas.[34] In 2005, Russian frustration with the US presence grew, as the US appeared to endorse the overthrow of Kyrgyzstan's president, Askar Akayev, in the most recent of the 'colour revolutions', which the US viewed as a democratic revolution, but which Moscow saw as a dangerous destabilisation of the country and potentially the entire region. At the summit of the Shanghai Cooperation Organisation (SCO) in 2005, the final communiqué called upon the US to commit to a schedule for withdrawal:[35] Russia was reportedly the driving force behind this message.[36] Subsequently, Russia moved aggressively to fill the diplomatic vacuum left by the rift in US–Uzbek relations in 2005 and America's expulsion from its Uzbek air base.[37]

But the country's more recent posture in Central Asia has hinted at its continuing interest in a US presence in Afghanistan and in US assistance in securing Central Asia from the threat of the re-Talibanisation of its unstable neighbour. The 2006 and 2007 SCO communiqués did not appeal for a US military withdrawal from the region. Moreover, despite persistent rumours, Russia has not expanded its military presence in Central Asia and has apparently resisted calls from the region to do so,[38] focusing its activity instead on pipelines and energy diplomacy and countering US and European schemes in those areas instead. It seems likely that the deterioration of the security environment in Afghanistan has had a dampening effect on Russian diplomacy aimed at reducing the US military presence and consolidating Russian influence in Central Asia.

Stopping the production and flow of drugs from Afghanistan has emerged in recent years as a particular shared interest between Russia and the US and its allies, albeit one that currently expresses itself mainly in Russia's frustration with what it sees as NATO's ineffectiveness in the face of the problem. Russian policymakers and analysts have been complaining that the flow of drugs from Afghanistan poses an increasing threat to Russia as a transit country, and one with a growing population of addicts. Russian Deputy Foreign Minister Sergei Kislyak has called for an 'anti-drug security belt' to be put around Afghanistan.[39] It remains to be seen whether a common interest in tackling the narcotics trade will result in Russian–Western cooperation on this issue.

Events in Afghanistan more broadly could influence relations between Russia and the West in a number of different directions over the coming months and years. Russia's acquiescence in the presence of the US and its allies in Central Asia, as the price to be paid for securing the region from the threat of re-Talibanisation, is likely to be in inverse proportion to its assessment of the success of US and Coalition efforts in Afghanistan: should the situation there improve, Russian activity aimed at terminating the US military presence in Central Asia is likely to be stepped up; should it remain precarious, Russia is likely to continue to tolerate the US presence in its Central Asian hinterland.

However, should the situation deteriorate to the point where Moscow feels that a US and Coalition presence is no longer a major factor in Afghan security, Russian interest in keeping the US in the region could well disappear altogether, and Russia may then move to take the region's security into its own hands.

The third Central Asian development, the expanding presence of China in the region, is one of the most important challenges on Russia's strategic agenda. Many in the Russian strategic community believe that China's rise threatens Russian interests in Asia – from the Far East, where Russia's population and military capabilities have been declining as a result of the state's unwillingness to shoulder the financial burden associated with them, to Central Asia, where China's economic dynamism is proving irresistible to the local economy.[40] Russia's interests vis-à-vis China are discussed below; their relevance here is that in Central Asia, the US presence serves another important Russian interest: helping Moscow balance Beijing's growing influence.

b) Iran

There is little doubt that US and European assessments of Iran differ from Russian assessments of that country. Russian policy toward Iran has been the subject of considerable differences between Russia and the US and its European allies on numerous occasions. However, the US, Russia and Europe also have a number of interests vis-à-vis Iran that ultimately coincide, the most prominent of which is the nuclear issue, treated below.

Russian interests in Iran are diverse. Over the years, Iran has been a reliable buyer of Russian arms – combat aircraft, tanks, air-to-air and surface-to-air missiles and other hardware.[41] In addition, Russia has for many years been building a nuclear power plant at Bushehr in Iran. For a long time, the project was a sore point in relations between Russia and the US, because of American suspicions and allegations that the Bushehr programme, which Russia claims is strictly civilian, was a de facto conduit of know-how and technology for a covert Iranian nuclear-weapons programme. This has been consistently denied by Russian representatives, who insist that Russian nuclear cooperation with Iran is strictly peaceful and conforms to all International Atomic Energy Agency regulations.[42] In 2005, the US changed its policy and acquiesced in Bushehr, after Russia accepted additional safeguards on the project. This position was formalised in a letter from US President Bush to Putin in June of that year.[43]

Nevertheless, US sanctions against Russian companies accused of collaborating with Iranian nuclear weapons and missile programmes have reinforced Russia's resentment of what it sees as US unilateralism on the Iranian nuclear issue. This resentment has undoubtedly played a major part in shaping Russia's often cool attitude towards American assessments of Iran's intentions to develop such weapons. Russia does not share much of America's fear about Iranian nuclear weapons and ballistic missiles, as could be seen in its argument that US plans for a BMD system to protect Europe and the US from Iranian missiles were an overreaction.[44] Moreover, some Russian analysts have on occasion expressed the view that, were Iranian nuclear weapons to come into being, they would not pose a major threat to Russia and its interests, but would represent a major threat to the US and its interests, and thus would level a strategic playing field that has tilted in the US's favour.[45]

The prospect of an Iranian nuclear capability has not been high on Russia's national security agenda for other reasons as well. For much of the past decade-and-a-half, Russian policymakers have had many other, more pressing, mostly domestic, concerns to occupy them. The Russian security agenda has been dominated by the war in Chechnya and security problems in the North Caucasus. In that arena, Iran has proven a model partner to Russia, never criticising its policies there or intervening on behalf of the Chechens. Elsewhere where Russian security interests have been at stake, in Central Asia and Afghanistan, Iran and Russia have joined forces in opposition to the Taliban, and in Central Asia they have found common cause in opposing the US Caspian pipelines policy.

The relationship with Iran also provides Russia with an important entry point into Middle East politics, where, as we have seen, Russian opportunities to play a substantial role in regional affairs have declined significantly since the Cold War. Iran's growing ambitions and stature in

Middle East politics make it an increasingly important interlocutor for Russia, while the notion that Russia and Iran have a special relationship is seen by some in Moscow as having the potential to give Russia the status of a major power in the region, and perhaps even to make it an indispensable intermediary between the West and Iran.

However, the relationship between Russia and Iran is not free of its problems and contradictions, and Russian interests are not subordinate to it. First of all, Russian influence with Iran appears in practice to be quite limited, and Russian representatives have reportedly been growing frustrated with Iran.[46] Their efforts to persuade Iran to accept the 2005 US–EU–Russian compromise solution[47] to the stand-off over its nuclear programme, for example, came up short, demonstrating that the special relationship with Tehran in reality gives Moscow limited leverage at best.

While Russian officials and analysts may be less alarmed about Iranian nuclear ambitions than the Americans, they most likely are sincere in their stated desire to keep Iran from actually acquiring nuclear weapons.[48] This position is likely to be driven by concerns about possible US responses and their consequences for Russia.[49] Further destabilisation of the Middle East as a result of US military action against Iran would not be in Russia's interest, given Iran's proximity to Russia's southern borders.[50]

Moscow has taken a number of steps to communicate to Tehran that its patience has its limits. In December 2006 and again in March 2007,[51] it joined the US and the rest of the UN Security Council in a unanimous resolution to impose limited sanctions on Iran for refusing to stop its uranium-enrichment activities, having also previously voted in July 2006 with a Security Council resolution mandating a suspension of these activities.

By early 2007, reports were circulating that the state-owned Russian company building the Bushehr plant had suspended work because Tehran had fallen behind on its payments. Other reports suggested that Russia would not deliver fuel for the plant unless Iran suspended enrichment. There was also speculation that the construction company was falling behind schedule deliberately, in order to signal Russian displeasure with Iran's intransigence on the enrichment issue.[52]

Russian frustration with Iran may ultimately have positive consequences for the West, and for Russia itself. Russia has far-reaching plans to become a leading supplier of nuclear fuel worldwide; supplying, reprocessing and storing spent nuclear fuel for the industry, which is currently undergoing a revival. Russia stands to benefit financially from participating in the Global Nuclear Energy Partnership[53] proposed by the US, which would supply countries with advanced nuclear recycling and reactor technologies in exchange for pledges to forego enrichment and reprocessing facilities. This initiative is likely to prove far more lucrative to Russia than the remainder of the Bushehr project.[54] In 2007, a civilian nuclear cooperation agreement was negotiated between the US and Russia to enable Russian participation in the partnership – hitherto, Russian cooperation with Iran had been a major impediment to such a deal, but Russia's toughening stance vis-à-vis Iran and improved US–Russian cooperation on this issue led the Bush administration in the US to push the agreement ahead.[55]

Though Iran and Russia have long found themselves in shared opposition to US- and European-backed plans for oil and gas pipelines between the Caspian and Europe, oil, gas and related infrastructure issues may also become an area of tensions between Moscow and Tehran in the future. In the Caspian itself for example, while Russia, Azerbaijan and Kazakhstan have reached agreements on the boundaries between their sectors of the sea, Iran and Turkmenistan have yet to agree to any proposed boundaries. This could become a contentious issue between Russia and Iran if Iran threatens oil and gas projects in disputed waters where Russian companies have a stake. As exporters of oil and gas, the two countries may in the future also find themselves competing for a share of European markets, or pursuing competing pipeline projects, as worldwide demand for gas grows and such projects become more financially and technologically feasible for both countries.

In the long run, therefore, the relationship between Russia and Iran may in fact prove to be quite fraught. However, while Russia may further curtail its nuclear cooperation with Iran and eventually slightly downgrade the overall relationship, it is unlikely to want to alter it radically. Though commercial considerations may prove to be a powerful incentive for Moscow to move closer to the position of the US and Europe in regard to the nuclear issue, Russian policymakers will have to weigh the prospect of financial gains from cooperation with the US-promoted nuclear energy initiative against other major considerations: the importance of maintaining overall good relations with Iran and protecting other aspects of that relationship; the risk associated with accepting terms dictated by the US of once again being perceived as playing second fiddle to Washington; and Russia's interest in squeezing all the financial gains that can be wrought from the long-standing Bushehr project (which may turn out not to be compatible with involvement with the US fuel scheme, from either the Iranian or American points of view).

Russian frustration with Tehran's intransigence over the nuclear issue is likely to grow in the years to come, as it comes to be seen as imperilling

Russian security as it relates to the Middle East, and as standing in the way of Russia, as its ally, reaping the benefits of peaceful nuclear cooperation with countries opposed to the Iranian position. But given the high stakes and the countervailing factors identified above, this frustration is unlikely to prompt Moscow to make any sudden moves vis-à-vis either Tehran or Washington.

VI: Secondary, but increasingly important concerns

Alongside this extensive menu of Russian interests that define the strategic agenda vis-à-vis Europe and the United States, Moscow has a number of secondary concerns that have the potential to have a major impact on Russian attitudes towards the West in both the short and long term.

As Russia reaches new levels of prosperity, issues like visa requirements for Russian tourists travelling to Europe and the US, and restrictions on market access for Russian companies seeking to acquire assets in the US and EU, gain in prominence. These second-tier issues are intertwined with Russia's big-power aspirations and its desire for recognition as a major player in the international arena. As the country's economic clout increases and Russian capital and people become more mobile, Russian elites, the general public and government officials will find themselves more frequently in situations in which they are refused privileges that are generally available to citizens of other European nations, such as free passage into an EU country without additional documentation, or unfettered freedom to operate in a particular commercial market. This situation threatens to be viewed from the Russian side in terms of mistreatment and double standards.[56] Russians will be apt to dismiss European and American explanations of instances of perceived discrimination on the grounds of security or anti-monopoly considerations as cover for politically motivated singling out of Russian businesses and citizens, and a slight to Russia's prestige.

China – ally, for now
Currently, Russian–Chinese relations appear to be excellent and improving, with the two Eurasian powers jointly presiding over the SCO and professing a commonality of interests in Central Asia and elsewhere. However, as we have seen, their interests may not be as complementary as their declarations might suggest. Central Asia is only one of several areas in which Russian interests could come into conflict with those of China.

There is every indication that the relationship with China will in the long run rise to the top of Russia's foreign-policy agenda. This is commonly recognised by a wide range of Russian foreign-policy specialists.[57] At the beginning of this decade, the Council for Foreign and Defence Policy questioned whether Russia would be able to retain Siberia and the Far East as territories in the face of Chinese economic and strategic dynamism.[58] A more positive, but also sobering assessment of Russia's position vis-à-vis China was made by the same organisation in 2007, identifying as the leading 'risk' in the next decade Russia's ending up 'farther away from the West, especially from the United States and Europe, than from [China]. This [would] undercut its competitive advantages and weaken it politically'.[59]

Few Russian analysts and policymakers fail to acknowledge the disparity between Russian and Chinese economic and demographic strength, especially in the Russian Far East. President Putin summarised the prevalent feeling early in his tenure during a visit to Blagoveshchensk in the Far East in July 2000: 'If we don't make an effort, the Russian population here will be speaking in Japanese [and] Chinese'.[60]

Commenting on joint Russian–Chinese military exercises in 2005, leading Russian defence analyst and former Deputy Chairman of the Defence Committee of the Duma Aleksey Arbatov argued that militarily Russia was becoming China's junior partner. Tactically, he believed, this development could suit Russia, China being a major weapons export market for Russian manufacturers, but, he concluded, it was not in Russia's long-term interest. China might be the biggest buyer of Russian arms, but 'we are clearly getting carried away and it is absolutely obvious that China will do nothing for us'.[61]

The Russian Far East is falling victim to its economic weakness and the demographic predicament of the country at large. Population decline in the region is significant – the population was under seven million in 2005, and is projected to fall to below five million over the next two decades.[62] The overall labour shortage projected to hit Russia in the coming years[63] means that the Far East will face stiff competition to attract residents from other regions. The region's remoteness from European Russia, with underdeveloped road, rail and air links, contrasts with its proximity to a dynamic China that not only offers an endless supply of labour, but has the kind of economic gravitational pull that it will be difficult for Russia's most remote province to escape.

Russia's uncertainty about its interests in China and how it should handle China's ascendancy is reflected in its policymaking. Cordial political relations, weapons trading, phases of joint opposition to the US presence in Central Asia and more shared consistent opposition to a US-dominated unipolar world have seen Moscow and Beijing working more closely together in recent years, making the Sino-Soviet stand-off of the 1960s and 1970s a distant memory. At the same time, Russia is wary. In 2004–5, for instance, the Kremlin evidently had considerable trouble deciding whether to have the final section of an oil pipeline to the Pacific built across Chinese territory or confined to Russia. The former option was reportedly considerably less expensive, making it at face value the obvious choice. But concern about ensuring Russian control of this strategic resource drew the Kremlin instead towards the option of building in Russia. It is by no means clear that a final route has been agreed on, but it seems that some work has begun in Russia, with reported plans for a spur to Daqing in China.[64]

The difficulty of such decisions illustrates Russia's ambivalent approach to its powerful neighbour. With the correlation of forces heavily in favour of Beijing, Russia cannot afford not to have good relations with China, but ensuring a proper balance in the relationship between short-term interests and long-term considerations is clearly no easy task, and it will preoccupy Russian policymakers for the foreseeable future. There is widespread suspicion in Russia that China's enormous economic and demographic and, ultimately, military and strategic advantage means that getting close to it, though perhaps economically prudent in the short term, would in the long term hand substantial leverage to a nation willing and able, Russians fear, to thoroughly exploit it.

In the long run, then, Russian–Chinese relations look far from trouble-free, and an awareness of difficulties ahead may well steer Russian efforts westward in the medium term. The fragility of Russia's position in the East underscores the fact that the preponderance of Russian interest is in the West. Putin's famous threat, made in 2006, to send Russian oil and gas to Asia-Pacific instead of to Europe[65] because of what he claimed were unfair conditions faced by Russian energy companies in Europe appears rather hollow given Russia's strategic vulnerability vis-à-vis China, leaving aside the issue of what it might cost to build multiple new pipelines to the Pacific rim. Cultural affinities, too, may play a role in determining which way Russia most frequently faces in the future: in the words of First Deputy Prime Minister Sergei Ivanov, a close associate of Putin's and reportedly a leading contender to succeed him in 2008, 'on the whole, we are of course Europeans, not Asians'.[66]

CHAPTER THREE

The Domestic Political Setting

Putin's foreign policy, unlike that of his predecessor, has the advantage of a benign domestic political setting. It enjoys strong public support, reflecting a broad consensus that has emerged in Russian society and the Russian political elite alike.

Putin's personal popularity among his countrymen is well known. Public opinion polls consistently put his approval rating at well above 70%. At the time of writing, it was as high as 80%. This is undoubtedly an impressive accomplishment, especially in comparison to the low esteem in which his predecessor was held, and in view of the 'voter fatigue' that often affects the popularity of leaders who have been in office for a long period of time.

There is broad public approval of Putin's approach to all the major contemporary themes in Russian foreign relations and interests abroad, including relations with countries of the former Soviet Union and with Europe and the United States, energy trade and democracy promotion. Equally, Putin's stated and implicit positions on important internal issues such as the fate of the former Soviet Union, the record of the 1990s and the legacy of Boris Yeltsin also reflect prevailing popular attitudes.

Popular moves

When long-standing tensions between Russia and Georgia escalated in the autumn of 2006, Russian authorities ordered law-enforcement officials to detain ethnic Georgians residing or travelling in Russia without proper documents and deport them to Georgia. The highly publicised operation, which affected both Georgians and Russian citizens of Georgian extraction, as well as Georgian-owned and operated businesses in Russia, was widely criticised in the Western media,as well as by a number of independently minded media outlets in Russia.[1]

But the operation met with widespread support from the Russian public. Polls showed that 51% blamed the Georgian government and its 'provocative actions' for the crisis, while only 5% put the responsibility on the Kremlin. Those who accused Georgia of being a puppet of the United States numbered 44%; 33% believed it wanted to join NATO; and 23% that it wanted to remove Russian troops and bases from Georgia. Another 64% approved of the economic blockade Russia had imposed on Georgia; and 74% approved of increased scrutiny of and closures of Georgian-owned businesses in Russia. However, 71% opposed military action against Georgia.[2]

Such attitudes, and the Putin government's actions during this crisis, are not exceptional in the general landscape of Russian politics and public opinion. In 2005, the Russian government's policy toward Ukraine during the 'Orange Revolution' elicited supportive reactions from the general public. A substantial proportion of poll respondents – 48% – approved of Putin's policy of blunt intervention in the electoral process and support for the candidate deemed friendly to Moscow. Of the 24% who disapproved, 14% attributed any misjudgements to Putin's being wrongly informed by his aides. Those respondents who thought that Russia was more democratic than Ukraine numbered 45%, while only 12% thought the opposite. A further 23% believed that the Russian government's actions toward Ukraine were not tough enough.[3] In another poll, conducted in May 2006, nearly 70% of respondents said they believed that Ukraine's membership of NATO would pose at least some threat to Russia.[4]

In May 2007, Russian public opinion was stirred up by the Estonian government's decision to move the remains of Red Army soldiers buried in a central square in Tallinn to a military cemetery on the outskirts of town. The decision was widely covered in the Russian media and presented as the desecration of the memory of Soviet soldiers who fought against Nazi Germany. The Russian government's indignant rhetoric and action taken to 'punish' Estonia were broadly endorsed by the Russian public, of whom 60%, according to one poll taken during the crisis, believed that Estonia was Russia's 'number one' enemy (Georgia was in second place, with 46%).[5]

Impact of media manipulation

Of course, as major public information channels such as television are in one form or another controlled by or dependent on the Russian government, Russian public opinion is undoubtedly manipulated by government propaganda. It is also important to note, however, especially in a discussion of the domestic context of Russian foreign policy, that with regard to public information, Russia is not the Soviet Union, where all domestic media were tightly controlled and censored, and access to foreign media was almost completely denied to the general public. The rise of the Internet has provided unprecedented opportunities for the Russian public to gain access to numerous Russian- and foreign-language publications, which report news and opinion from a wide variety of domestic and foreign sources. Moreover, there are several websites devoted to the rapid and accurate translation of foreign-language news and commentary from and about Russia, including of reports and opinion pieces very unfavourable towards the government.[6]

While Internet use is still in the relatively early stages of development in Russia, and lags far behind most other European countries, the importance of electronic media in Russia should not be dismissed as insignificant because they do not reach an audience as large as that of television. According to a public opinion poll conducted at the end of 2006, 22% of Russian households had a personal computer, and 35% of respondents reported using a computer at least once a week; 28% reported accessing the Internet (besides using email) at least once a week.[7] In September 2006, the popular Russian internet portal Yandex released a survey showing that there were well over a million Russian-language blogs.[8]

So while the Russian public is certainly subject to a substantial dose of government propaganda, it is no longer dependent on government-controlled media for access to information about events in the country and abroad. This is the context in which we should view the popularity of Russia's international posture with its citizens.

Putin articulates what many Russians feel and believe. When he said in his annual address to the Federal Assembly in April 2005 that the collapse of the USSR was the 'greatest geopolitical catastrophe of the twentieth century',[9] he shocked many in Europe and the US, where the demise of the Soviet Union was greeted with hope and relief. However, to many Russians, the break-up of the USSR represents a tragedy, an event that marked the end of a great power in whose service so many of their ancestors had laboured and died. A survey taken in late 2006 showed 61% regretting the demise of the USSR and 59% who thought it could have been avoided. Few, however, (18%) believed it could be brought back.[10]

A poll conducted in 2005 during the twentieth anniversary of perestroika revealed that 56% of respondents thought that perestroika had
played a negative role in the life of the country. When the data was broken
down by age, this assessment was shown to be widely held across age categories. 35% thought that if it hadn't been for perestroika, Russian living
conditions would have slowly improved, and 36% believed that 'one great
country would have been preserved'.[11]

Perhaps with this regret in mind, Russian citizens consistently express
strong support for Putin's tough handling of Russia's relationships with the
former Soviet republics. In December 2005, a poll was taken in which 80%
of respondents favoured raising gas prices for Ukraine, a highly controver-
sial policy that was widely criticised in the US and Europe.[12]

The purpose of citing these statistics is not to provide an exhaustive
account of Russian public opinion on all aspects of Putin's foreign policy
and Russia's position in the world. Rather, it is to give chapter-and-verse
evidence of the extent to which Putin's foreign policy, his vision of Russian
interests abroad and his choice of means to advance those interests have
enjoyed the broad and consistent support of his constituents.

The democracy issue

This discussion should not be construed to be making any judgements
about the quality of Russian democracy on Putin's watch as compared to
that of the Yeltsin era. Russian democracy is a subject that is too large and
complex to be addressed adequately within the confines of this study.

However, the theme of a Russian retreat from democracy has emerged
as one of the most contentious issues in relations between Russia and the
West. The charge that Russia is becoming more undemocratic is one that
Russian government representatives, including Putin himself, vehemently
deny, maintaining that Russia is building its own brand of tough 'sovereign'
democracy, which safeguards Russia from damaging foreign influence,
protects its interests and enables it to avoid the kind of chaos that plagued
the country throughout the 1990s. And indeed, to the extent that the task
of maintaining stability requires limited constraints on personal freedoms,
Russian citizens appear to be quite content to accept this trade-off. The
freewheeling era of Boris Yeltsin gets bad marks in Russian public opinion
polls.[13]

A vigorous Russian response to Western charges of a retreat from
democracy has been accompanied in recent years by policies aimed
at curtailing foreign influence on domestic politics. The law on non-
governmental organisations (NGOs) that was enacted in 2006[14] imposed

rigid new registration requirements on foreign NGOs and created new mechanisms for monitoring both foreign and domestic NGOs. Government allegations that foreign intelligence organisations use Russian NGOs for their nefarious purposes[15] and other accusations about NGO purposes have evidently been intended to convince the public that outsiders seeking to promote democracy and civil society in Russia do not have the country's best interests in mind.

Dissatisfactions

Despite broad Russian acquiescence in the Kremlin's actions in relation to foreign democracy advocates, as well as in the other policies discussed above, public opinion data also suggests something else, that is not widely acknowledged by senior Russian officials, yet is likely to have a lot to do with their firmly negative response to foreign democracy promotion activities inside Russia. Despite Putin's consistently high personal approval ratings, poll after poll leaves very little room for doubt that the stability in which he and his aides take such pride rests on a rather precarious foundation.

Public opinion polls show a big gap between Putin's personal popularity on the one hand, and Russian voters' confidence in and approval of the policies of his government and of the government in itself, on the other. For example, in November 2006, Putin's overall approval rating stood at 77%; Prime Minister Mikhail Fradkov's at 44%; and the government's as a whole at 40%. 44% of respondents said they believed the country was on the wrong path, while only 38% thought it was on the right path. 65% expressed dissatisfaction with the general state of affairs in the country, 63% disapproved of the government's economic policy and 81% disapproved of the country's moral climate.[16]

Russian citizens have a wide range of complaints to make against their government and its policies. The government appears to them to be unable to deal with unemployment, inflation, the meagre provision of social benefits and social inequality. Various state institutions – the police, prosecutors, the security services – are seen as caring only about their own gain or that of the government, and as doing nothing in the interest of the common folk. Russia's citizens have lost trust in the police, courts and local government, and the majority of them feel that they are defenceless before the authorities. Russian voters' dissatisfaction with their country's domestic condition runs deep and stands in stark contrast with the highly favourable opinion they seem to have of President Putin himself.

The Russian public has much to be disillusioned about. The rapid economic growth of the Putin era has certainly produced its winners. The wealthy Russians who sail their yachts in the Mediterranean, buy castles in Scotland and throw opulent parties in Europe's trendiest ski resorts are there for all to see in the gossip pages of Russian newspapers.[17] But the rising tide of the Russian economy has not lifted all boats. One in three polled in 2006 described their economic situation as 'bad' or 'very bad'. More than half described the situation in the region where they lived as 'tense' or even 'explosive'. Fewer than 15% wanted the results of privatisation conducted in the 1990s to be allowed to remain.[18]

This is not a happy electorate or a recipe for domestic tranquillity. Many Russians are filled with a sense of injustice and want someone to be held accountable for their misfortunes. The question of 'who is guilty?' in Russian politics, asked in the nineteenth century by the great Russian revolutionary writer Aleksandr Gertsen, has yet to be definitively answered.

Considering the degree of dissatisfaction among the Russian public, it should come as no surprise that the political elite huddled around the president views the situation in the country with unease. The prospect of Putin's departure generates a deep uncertainty, normal in the context of any political succession, but compounded in this instance by the fact that the mechanism of succession is new and untested, the result cannot be guaranteed, and, unfortified by the presence of Putin himself, the Kremlin's systems for projecting its power could prove to be less effective than many in the government might like.

The 'vertical of power'

Putin has invested a great deal of energy throughout his presidency in the construction and strengthening of the so-called 'vertical of power'. This is the literal translation of a Russian term that has been widely used inside and outside Russia to denote Putin's notion of a top-down system by which a strong central government is able to swiftly and firmly transmit policy and instructions from the Kremlin throughout the various layers of federal, regional and local government, and ensure the prompt enforcement of its decisions. But after considerable efforts have been put into making sure that the chief executive's influence is felt at each level of decision-making, and officials at all levels are accountable to him (for instance, through the appointment of Kremlin representatives to oversee provincial governors, and making governors directly answerable to the president), the 'vertical of power' has emerged as a rather unstable construct. By expanding the reach of the presidency and making officials accountable to the Kremlin, rather than to their electorates, Putin has effectively narrowed the executive branch's support base and made it highly dependent on his personal popularity. Instead of expanding his and his government's support base, he has created something akin to an inverted pyramid in which the foundation – the vast government bureaucracy – rests on the pyramid's tip – Putin.

In these circumstances it is clear why Russia's political elites have responded so negatively to American and European support for democratic movements in nearby former Soviet states, as well as in Russia proper. The 'colour revolutions' that led to the overthrow of entrenched, long-serving governments in Georgia, Ukraine and, in 2005, Kyrgyzstan, have had uncomfortable resonances for Russia's political class. Aside from bringing about chaos in Kyrgyzstan and NATO- and EU-friendly governments in Ukraine and Georgia, the colour revolutions are seen by the Kremlin as threatening Russia's own stability, with the support of Westerners eager to destabilise Russia in the name of democracy.

There are likely to be few illusions in the minds of the country's political establishment about the effectiveness of the 'vertical of power' or the degree to which modern-day Russia can in fact be controlled from the Kremlin. The notion that Russia has reverted to its totalitarian past, which one might infer from the Western media reports and commentaries critical of policies such as the elimination of elections to provincial governorships and the Kremlin's control of major media outlets, does not reflect the reality of today's Russia, with its expanding internet use, growing number of mobile phone users (which recently exceeded the number of residents in the country[19]), and unprecedented popular access to foreign travel. The lack of confidence among Russia's elite in the effectiveness of the 'vertical of power' and the government's ability to respond to crises and control the situation in the country is reflected in the elite's resentment of and opposition to Western attempts to promote democracy in Russia and its vicinity. Members of Russia's political class are likely to view these attempts as a challenge to the country's domestic stability, which they believe the government is ill-equipped to handle.

'Sovereign democracy' and self-respect

The doctrine of 'sovereign democracy', articulated most notably by Putin's deputy chief of staff, Vladislav Surkov, is the Kremlin's answer to the challenge of democracy promotion from abroad and the prospect of spontaneous domestic destabilisation. A central element of this doctrine is the idea that Russian domestic affairs are for Russians to manage, not for foreigners to dictate. The people of Russia, the doctrine runs, will determine for themselves what type of democracy they want to create and consolidate in their own country. Foreign attempts to promote democracy in Russia constitute an affront to the Russian people because they are a gross violation of their nation's sovereignty.[20]

With this concept, the Kremlin appeals to the wounded pride and sense of compromised sovereignty that many in Russia retain from the 1990s, when the country was unable to stand on its own and declare its interests with a clear and dignified voice. This reminder of the mismatch between the memory that many Russians have of the 1990s as a period of chaos, and their celebration by foreign commentators as a time when democracy blossomed, reinforces the negative connotations in the public's mind of foreign democracy promoters, their associates inside Russia, and their criticisms of Putin's mode of governing, his 'sovereign democracy'. Foreign government and NGO support for domestic Russian pro-democracy movements and organisations tends in this climate to have the effect of making the latter appear treacherous, content to compromise Russian sovereignty in exchange for handouts of foreign aid.

Putin has frequently countered foreign questioning of his domestic record with appeals to Russian sovereignty, dignity and self-respect. For example, while visiting Austria in May 2007, he responded to a reporter's question about Western criticism of Russia's lacklustre record on democratic development by saying that Russia was ready to address these issues together with other countries, but that it would not stand for anyone lecturing it or telling it what to do.[21] In his annual address to the Federal Assembly in the previous month, Putin had also said that:

> The stream of foreign money used for direct interference in our internal affairs is growing. If [we] look at what was happening in the past, we will see that during the colonial era [they] talked about the civilising mission of colonial powers. Today [they] are armed with democratisation slogans. But the goal is the same – to gain one-sided advantages and benefits, [advance] one's own interests.[22]

'Sovereign democracy' appears to resonate well with the Russian public. A survey conducted in 2006 showed a 56% majority supporting increased government control of the media, against only 21% opposing it. Russians supported restrictions on foreign NGOs engaged in the promotion of human rights by a 43:32 margin. 44% favoured the 'Chinese model' of development; strong central government combined with economic dynamism, as against 30% favouring 'liberal democracy'.[23]

While such statistics might suggest that the Russians are inherently undemocratic, there is equally impressive polling data to show that Russian voters have a healthy respect for democratic values. For example, a survey conducted in the spring of 2007 revealed that Russians supported by an overwhelming margin – 75:11 – the right of opposition parties and movements to protest publicly; and that they did not believe that the government had the right to ban such marches (64:21), or that the government should use force to disband them (65:19).[24] It is instructive to note that a 66% majority of those polled were not even aware of the opposition protests conducted in March 2007.[25] The lack of information about protest events appears to be part of a deliberate government strategy to isolate the opposition, in line with the authoritarian elements of 'sovereign democracy'.

'Russia's apolitical middle'

Despite high levels of dissatisfaction with the government's policies and the country's overall predicament, and officials' fears of instability, there appears in fact to be little appetite for political action or wholesale political change among the general public. Whenever incidents of mass protest have occurred in recent years, they have usually been triggered either by fairly specific financial issues, such as the government's decision to monetise pensions in 2005,[26] or by ethnic tensions, as in the case of the disturbances in the city of Kondopoga in Northwest Russia in the autumn of 2006, which were sparked by a violent incident between Russians and Chechens.[27] In both these instances the federal government reacted swiftly to contain the protests, in the first case by allocating additional funds, in the second by deploying police reinforcements to the area. Neither protest offered much basis for broader political mobilisation. For the time being, many Russian citizens – 'Russia's apolitical middle' in the words of one prominent critic of Putin's policies[28] – being tired of upheavals, seem happy choosing stability over liberal democracy and its attendant uncertainty.

Nationalism – how great a threat?

Some observers have discerned a deviation from this tendency. Commentators, Russian and foreign, have noted with alarm the presence of racism and radical nationalism inside Russia[29] and the Putin government's tendency to manipulate this to its advantage.[30]

Presently, Russian nationalism appears to be a largely top-down phenomenon, and, while the authorities happily rely on aggressive nationalist rhetoric when it is expedient, as in the case of the sanctions imposed on ethnic Georgians, they have jealously guarded against spontaneous actions driven by nationalist ideologies that could lead to broader political mobilisation. For example, the nationalist Rodina movement, reportedly created by the Kremlin to undercut the Communist Party in the 2003 parliamentary elections, was subsequently manipulated into political irrelevance by the Kremlin once it appeared to gain a political momentum of its own and no longer served the interests of its creators.[31] How long the government will be able to control such movements is an important question, but its ability to do so is certainly enhanced by the state's permissive application of the rule of law, which is unlikely to change any time soon.[32]

Nationalism as it is reflected in Russian public opinion at large is of a relatively passive kind. There appears to be relatively little grassroots support for extreme nationalist ideologies; the more prominent nationalist organisations are, more often than not, creatures of the Kremlin, which rarely survive beyond their usefulness to it. Russians may express strong support for Putin's policies towards Georgia and Ukraine, but very few would endorse the notion of military action in the name of restoring the Russian empire. Russian citizens may be nostalgic for the Soviet era when they were citizens of a superpower, but, as we have seen, very few believe that the Soviet Union can be restored. Support for the idea of terminating gas deliveries to Georgia or Ukraine is largely based on narrow pecuniary self-interest, rather than any grand nationalist ambitions: why should Russia sell cheap gas to Ukraine and Georgia when so many Russians are still struggling to make ends meet? Why not squeeze all that we can from them?

Most Russians are, consistent with the 'apolitical middle' model of Russian citizenry, indifferent to all types of political ideology. Preoccupation with day-to-day survival; ideology fatigue after the failed promises of Soviet communism; disillusionment with the democracy–free market experiment of the 1990s; and the lack of credible political parties to articulate ideas and platforms for action all contribute to this indifference.[33]

Aggressive nationalism, though co-opted and instigated by the Kremlin domestically on occasion, and discernible in Russia's actions towards its ex-dominions, does not – at least yet – play a role in Russian participation in the forums of the major powers. Russia is not a revolutionary power in international relations. Though extreme nationalism may play well in some quarters in Russia, in the international arena, it motivates Russia to seek recognition in the international system, not to disrupt it. Russian leaders talk about a multipolar world, about the balance of power and interest, not a unipolar world revolving around Russia. Russia is still seeking recognition as a major power, a star in the constellation, and its leaders are hardly intent on destroying that constellation.

A domestic foundation

Russia could however – at least in its rhetoric – be described as a revisionist power with respect to what its foreign-policy and other political elites consider to be unfair changes in the international system brought about by Moscow's weakness during the 1990s. Key among these is the new European security architecture built around NATO. Russian leaders, as we have seen, are determinedly opposed to NATO's expansion further east. They seem equally determined to demonstrate to those ex-Soviet and Warsaw Pact states who have already joined NATO that there is a price to pay for disregarding Russian concerns, as illustrated by the tense relations between Russia and its Baltic neighbours and Poland. However, Moscow does not seem prepared to push this approach to the point of seeking the reversal of NATO's eastward expansion.

From the standpoint of its leaders, Russia is still on the defensive. In its pursuit of restoration as a major power, it is being forced to contend with two other powers that have the potential not only to damage Russia's international standing, but also to upset its domestic tranquillity on a revolutionary scale. America's pursuit of democracy threatens both Russia's legitimacy in the international arena and its domestic status quo. China represents a challenge of a very different kind, whose full implications have yet to be understood and adapted to, but one that many observers in Russia fear could result in major threats to Russia's position in Eurasia and even, in the long run, its territorial integrity. This pressure from the East tempts Russia westward, yet equally the country's newfound wealth and stability demand that it does not risk subordinating itself to undermining influences from the West. Russia has a delicate balance to maintain, at home and internationally. Russian leaders have therefore resorted to a form of 'managed' nationalism as a foundation for continued domestic support and national solidarity. How long and how successfully will they be able to preserve this foundation? The answer is likely to depend on the material resources at their disposal; on Russian economic performance and global economic conditions. Considering Russia's overall macroeconomic health, which will be discussed below, and – most importantly – assuming an on-balance favourable outlook for its performance as an exporter of oil, gas and various minerals and commodities (despite some dark clouds on that horizon), the domestic status quo, and the context it provides for Russian foreign policy, is likely to be maintained for the foreseeable future.

CHAPTER FOUR

The Economic Picture

As Putin delivered what he declared would be his final address on the state of the nation to the Russian parliament and the nation in April 2007, he might well have repeated the words traditionally uttered by his American counterparts: 'The state of our union is strong'. The country that Putin is preparing to leave to his successor is different in very many ways from the country he inherited from Boris Yeltsin.

The revival

Few readers will be unaware of Russia's spectacular comeback from the economic and political nadir that followed the collapse of the country's finances in 1998. All the same, it is instructive to cite some key facts. Recent figures on Russia's macroeconomic performance have made Russia the envy of many foreign central bankers and finance ministers, and paint a very different scene from the hopeless economic picture shortly after 1998. In 2006, the economy grew by nearly 7% – the eighth straight year of growth – and the federal budget had a surplus of 9% of GDP. During the previous five years, personal incomes grew by more than 12% per year in real terms; investment by 10% per year. Poverty declined steadily over the same period. Foreign currency reserves, as we have seen, currently stand at over $400 billion, and $22bn in debts to Paris Club creditor nations has been paid off. Inflation, at the end of 2006, stood at below 10%. The country's 'stabilisation fund', set up by the government in case of future financial upheavals, contains over $100bn. Additional reserve funds are also being set up for the same purpose. Foreign investors have been clamouring to put money into the Russian economy, with an estimated $28–30bn entering the country in foreign direct investment in 2006 – around double the figure for 2005.[1]

The Russian government has pursued a prudent financial policy, keeping firm control of expenditures, and Putin appears to be focused on making sure that his successor continues in this vein. Indeed the government is reported to have adopted a three-year budgetary framework so restrictive that it will leave Putin's successor very little room for any financial recklessness.[2]

There can be little doubt that in the eyes of Russia's leaders, as well as many of its citizens and outsiders, all this adds up to an important achievement — not only the restoration of Russia's economic health, but also the country's re-emergence from a long period of decline, retreat and dependence on external actors; a return to sovereignty and the freedom to pursue its own course in the international arena, charted by its own leaders, not world financial institutions or other international organisations. Russia does not need prompting from outsiders, 'cheat-sheets from the sidelines' in the words of Sergei Ivanov,[3] to answer the key questions about its direction at home and abroad: it is following its own script.

Global ambitions of an 'energy superpower'

The Russian president's pride in these achievements and confidence in his country's economic stature is such that he has even put forth an ambitious proposal to recast the global financial system in accordance with the new realities. The global financial system is still built around the G7 countries; this, Putin observed in a speech at the International Economic Forum in St Petersburg in June 2007, is a reflection of the situation that existed 50 years ago, when the G7 countries accounted for 60% of the world's GDP. In 2007, 60% of the world's GDP is produced outside the G7 countries. This change, Putin went on to say, calls for a new 'architecture of … international economic relations'.[4]

This appeal for a fundamental restructuring of the global financial architecture, regardless of whether or not it is eventually followed up with concrete proposals for action, is interesting for several reasons. Despite the evident satisfaction Putin derives from Russia's regained recognition as a major power and bona fide member of the world's most elite club of nations, the G8, in calling for this reform, he did not identify Russia with other members of that club. Rather, he chose to focus his remarks on the G7, thus juxtaposing Russia and other rising economic powerhouses against the established dominant Western powers that make up the G7.

This positioning of Russia and its interests by Putin can be read as another sign that, having arrived economically, Russia is not content to be a mere 'joiner', just another country that will play by rules that, in the view of Russian policymakers, were not made by the invisible hand of the marketplace, but by the powers who got in on the ground floor of globalisation and wrote the rulebook in accordance with their own interests and perceptions.

Putin's declaration in St Petersburg was also another indication of how different Russian foreign policy and its motivations have turned out to be from what was expected of Russia when it emerged from the Soviet Union. The notion that, in a globalised world, worldwide market forces would come to dictate the domestic actions and foreign postures of nations has certainly not been borne out by Russia's international behaviour or the claims that it makes on the international system. Instead, consistent with its balance-of-power-and-interests approach to foreign policy, Russia is re-emerging on the world economic stage guided by a mercantilist vision founded on its mineral wealth, a geographic position that gives it control of important trade routes, and the fact that most of its neighbours need the resources Russia either owns or controls. This vision has manifested itself most notably in the articulation by leading members of the country's political establishment of the concept of Russia as an 'energy superpower' – a major presence in the international arena whose prominence and special status are derived from its hydrocarbon wealth and the global economy's dependence on it.[5]

'National projects'

The Russian economic revival is certainly not only due to the worldwide increase in oil and gas prices and the resulting growth in oil and gas exports. Since the crisis of 1998, Russia has experienced growth in a number of export-oriented and domestic industries, in particular in mineral extraction and processing, retail, construction and food processing.[6] However, oil and gas exports have indisputably been the flagship industries of the Russian economic revival, and in the eyes of Russia's leaders, who have gone to great lengths to consolidate these industries under state control, oil and gas are the backbone of the country's economy, and its future.

At the same time, reliance on oil and gas as the engines of Russia's economic growth was understood from the start to be an unreliable strategy that could leave the country too vulnerable to price fluctuations. Russia would need to leverage its energy wealth, and use oil and gas profits to create new industries and conditions favourable for foreign investment, to secure its prospects for sustainable development.[7] To this end, Putin has personally launched a series of state-funded 'national projects' to feed some of the country's new wealth into areas the government has identified as key to Russia's strategic wellbeing and its long-term development. These include health, demographics, education and nanotechnology,[8] the last of these receiving particular attention as an eye-catching investment to give the Russian economy a competitive advantage: a flagship 130bn-rouble (c. $5bn) fund for the development of nanotechnology was announced in 2007 with much fanfare.

Yet despite the ample funding and intense publicity lavished on national projects by the government, media and the president himself, the prospects and likely impact on the economy of these schemes remain uncertain, not least in view of the unimpressive track record of large-scale government-funded projects in Russia. And in the meantime, a number of indicators point to a rather less radiant present and future for the Russian economy than the statistics cited in the preceding paragraphs might suggest.

Current and future troubles

As we know, the economic successes of the past eight or so years have not benefited all Russians. Russia's macroeconomic indicators may indeed be the envy of G8 finance ministers and central bankers, but there are other indicators of its economic and social state during Putin's tenure that place Russia in the same bracket as much poorer countries.

Poverty rates in Russia, as Putin celebrated in his most recent annual address to the federal assembly, have declined substantially. However, income inequality remains a major problem, and many Russians are still struggling to make ends meet, recalling the 2006 poll in which one in three described their economic situation as 'bad' or 'very bad'.[9]

Russia's demographic predicament has been described by both Russian and foreign scholars as 'catastrophic', and it is one of the economy's most enduring Achilles heels.[10] The population of Russia has been dropping steadily since the day the Soviet Union broke up and Russia emerged as an independent country; from 151m in 1991 to 146m in 2000, 143m in 2005, and just over 141m in 2007. It is projected to decline to 134m by 2015 and continue falling indefinitely beyond that date.[11] Some of the longer-range forecasts predict that by 2050 the population of Russia will have declined to 100–110m.[12]

The major consequence of the demographic crisis for the economy is, of course, labour shortage, which has become especially acute in the context of the demands of the economic revival. Russia has addressed this shortage by opening its doors to millions of legal and illegal migrant workers, making it by some accounts the second largest employer of migrant labour in the world after the US. Russia is now estimated to be home to more than three million illegal immigrants, mostly from the countries of the former Soviet Union, where economic conditions are forcing them to seek employment abroad.[13] As the population continues to shrink, Russia will become ever more reliant on foreign labour.[14] Shortages of skilled labour will become particularly severe, with a recent estimate predicting that in skilled construction, the deficit will be more than 20%; in computer programming, 19%; in finance, 14%; and in agriculture 7%. To compound the problem, in some areas, notably high-tech industry, Russia is losing skilled workers because they are able to command better terms of employment elsewhere.[15]

There are other negative indicators. Overall life expectancy at birth in Russia is estimated at 65 years, lower than in Brazil and China (both 72) and India (68). For Russian males, it is only 59. The infant mortality rate is 11 deaths per 1000 births,[16] well above the rates of other industrialised nations. Russia has some of the world's highest mortality rates for diseases of the circulatory system and for injury and poisoning; higher than those of its fellow former Soviet countries, let alone than those of Europe and the US.[17] To add more grim data to this already bleak picture, Russia is expected to be hit hard by an HIV/AIDS epidemic in the coming decade. A US National Intelligence Council report published in 2002 projected Russia to be one of the next sites of an HIV/AIDS epidemic, along with Ethiopia, Nigeria, India and China.[18] These problems have not gone unnoticed by the Russian government, which maintains that appropriate funds are allocated to healthcare; but clearly this hardly addresses the gravity of the problem.

Putin has broached the subject of the country's demographic crisis in speeches and has urged the government to design and implement urgent programmes to address the situation.[19] But the nature and magnitude of this crisis and its underlying conditions – decades of neglect of and under-investment in the country's social infrastructure, compounded by the socio-economic dislocation of the 1990s – are such that it is likely to remain as one of the most intractable problems faced by Russia and its economy.[20]

Income inequality, which Putin acknowledged in his 2007 federal assembly address, has a strongly regional character in Russia. The Human Development Index (HDI) of some of Russia's most prosperous regions, such as Moscow for example, competes with that of some countries in the

EU, such as Malta and the Czech Republic. But the HDI of Russia's poorest regions is comparable to that of some of the poorest nations in the world – Tajikistan, Mongolia and Guatemala.[21] According to the World Bank, in 2004 (the most recent year for which data is available) the GDP per capita of Russia's 10 most prosperous regions was four times greater than that of the 10 poorest regions.[22]

The situation has been worsening: according to the United Nations Development Programme, the gap between Russia's poorer and wealthier regions, as reflected in their life expectancy and per capita income, grew wider between 2002 and 2004.[23] Some regions have enjoyed a booming economy as a result of the economic revival, while others have stagnated. Economic growth during the current recovery has been distributed mainly in central, southern and southwestern Russia, and in resource-rich regions, such as oil-rich Tyumen. The World Bank predicts that regional disparities such as these are likely to increase further in the future.[24]

Regional socio-economic inequality goes hand-in-hand with poor infrastructure. The deterioration of Russia's roads has been widely reported in the Russian media: transport infrastructure has never been a strong point, but in recent years the problems have intensified. The extent of paved roads in the country declined by 50,000 kilometres between 2002 and 2005[25] due to poor maintenance and a slow rate of building (in 2000, 6,000km of new roads for cars were reported to have been built; in 2005, only 2,200km of such new roads were reported).[26]

In addition to these apparently endemic socio-economic and infrastructural problems, the Russian economy also has a poor business and investment climate, contrasting sharply with the conditions commonly expected to be found in G8 countries. In 2006, it stood in 121st place among 163 countries ranked in Transparency International's Corruption Perceptions Index, alongside Rwanda, Swaziland and the Philippines.[27] In a 2007 survey of property rights, it ranked 63rd of 70, comparable to Venezuela and Pakistan.[28] However, this climate does not appear to have had much of an impact on the flow of foreign investment, which, as we have seen, has increased dramatically in recent years, albeit from a relatively low base.

Financial opportunities afforded by the economic revival itself, including by this comparatively enthusiastic foreign investment and by the energy trade, have been missed. The early ambitions to use the gains from Russia's mineral wealth to finance reindustrialisation and the re-capitalisation of new sectors of the economy appear not to have been realised after nearly a decade of steadily rising energy revenues. Russia is instead using its commodities-fuelled economic recovery to finance its extractive sectors above all. The World Bank has estimated that in 2006, more than 33% of foreign direct investment went to industries dedicated to the extraction of mineral resources. The manufacturing sector received 19%, and it seems that nearly half of this was directed to metals (effectively an extension of the extractive sector) and food, which was mostly for domestic consumption, not export.[29] There is no indication in the statistics on foreign direct investment that Russia's economic revival and the attendant investment boom might spark reindustrialisation or the re-capitalisation of new export sectors.

The state of the major export industries: defence

While turning a far more modest profit than energy, arms exports are also important to the economy, generating an $8bn income in 2006.[30] In contrast with the fairly slim order book of the domestic defence industry, arms-export contracts worth $30bn were also reported in 2006, most with clients in Asia: in recent years, China and India in particular have become major purchasers of Russian weapons and equipment.[31]

However, despite a record-breaking volume of exports in 2006, the outlook for the Russian defence industry is not good. In the unanimous opinion of independent Russian and foreign experts, the industry is facing the problem of obsolescence on a large scale, and is currently surviving largely on old capital: research, development and production facilities have been starved of new investment ever since the Soviet economy went into a tailspin at the end of the 1980s.[32]

Moreover, as both Russian and foreign commentators have pointed out, in the not-so-distant future Russia will have to compete for markets in China and India against these countries' own arms industries, which are rapidly developing.[33] The EU's plans to sell weapons to China are also expected to hurt the Russian arms trade.[34] Diminishing Russian arms sales to China and India will have negative consequences not only for the Russian defence industry, but also for the Russian military, who need their primary source of equipment to be financially buoyant enough to be able to manufacture to a reasonably high standard.

The task of addressing large-scale industrial obsolescence needs urgently to be tackled by Russian defence industry leaders, who maintain that it is already underway.[35] It will be a long-term challenge, as Russian defence analysts believe the industry is effectively collapsing.[36] Prospects are discouraging: the industry's record on innovation is not good, and past efforts to reform the way it operates have reportedly made matters worse.[37]

The parlous state of Russia's defence industry and the prospect of declining sales to China and India are likely to make Russian exporters more aggressive in seeking access to new markets and protecting their share of existing ones. The recent reorganisation of major state-owned defence-industry and arms-exporting companies into one megaholding directly accountable to the president ought to give the arms lobby the muscle it needs to exercise an even greater influence over government policy in the area of arms exports.[38] Russia is likely to act forcefully in the future to protect its market share worldwide.

The state of the major export industries: energy

In trade, as in Russia's overall economic development, the extractive industries predominate. Oil, fuel and gas account for nearly 65% of Russian exports; metals nearly 14%; chemicals 6%; and machinery and equipment 6%.[39] Energy exports were worth nearly $200bn in 2006,[40] dwarfing all of Russia's other export industries. More than half of Russian trade is with Europe. 65% of Russian exports to the European Union are of energy/ mineral fuels; all other Russian exports pale in comparison with the energy trade between Russia and the EU.[41]

At the outset of Russia's economic revival, and for some time after it got underway, the reciprocal dependence on Russia of its trading partners in Europe, where deliveries from Russia account for nearly a quarter[42] of gas supply, was expected to foster a sense of partnership rooted in this dependence. The vast volume of energy trade would, it was thought, lead to pragmatic mutual accommodation.[43] As it has turned out, Europe's eagerness to wean itself off its dependence on Russian energy sources has motivated plans for the pipeline from Central Asia discussed above, which could well undermine Russia's export industry.

The importance of these exports to Russia has motivated it to redouble its efforts to consolidate and even expand its role in the European market in this context. The impulse to protect this trade lies at the heart of much Russian foreign policy and multiple foreign economic projects, including: the construction of a Baltic gas pipeline to link Russia directly with Germany, bypassing Belarus, Ukraine and Poland, by 2010; the row with Ukraine over gas prices and Russian concerns about Ukraine siphoning gas from the pipeline that transits the country on its way to Central and Western Europe; a Black Sea pipeline project; and, of course, the energy diplomacy in Central Asia aimed at consolidating Russian control over Central Asian gas exports and preventing them from reaching Europe by routes outside Russia.

Dealing with the gas deficit

Among the many challenges facing Russia on its current path of economic development, none is more significant in its potential impact than the depletion of Russian gas fields. Russia is already experiencing a short-fall in its gas production of approximately 60bn cubic metres of natural gas annually. It needs to produce 705bn cubic metres each year, of which roughly 400bn is for domestic consumption; 257bn for export; and 53bn to cover the requirements of Gazprom, the country's largest (and state-controlled) gas extraction company.[44] In 2005 and 2006, Gazprom produced 550bn cubic metres of gas each year, and independent Russian producers produced 95bn cubic metres in 2006; the shortfall was made up by imports from Central Asia. Russian forecasts suggest that this deficit is here to stay for the foreseeable future.[45]

According to Sergei Dubinin, former chairman of Russia's central bank and former deputy chairman of the board of Gazprom, the task of develop-ing enough new natural gas fields to cover the shortfall and bringing them online will be beyond Gazprom unless it can attract substantial outside investment, both foreign and domestic. In Dubinin's words, 'the epoch of cheap gas in Russia has ended'.[46] Estimates of the costs of developing new fields suggest that it will require a very aggressive new strategy on the part of Gazprom to attract the necessary investment.[47]

The importance of the gas trade to Russia might suggest a dynamic approach on the part of Russian policymakers and energy-sector leaders to the task of attracting investment in new fields. But this has not been forth-coming. The Russian government has instead increased and consolidated its control over the energy sector, while seeking to minimise the influ-ence of foreign companies in projects where they had previously played a leading role. For instance, in 2006, Shell was forced to yield its controlling interest in the Sakhalin-2 gas project to Gazprom. Similarly, under pres-sure from the Russian government, BP sold its stake in the Kovykta gas field to Gazprom in June 2007.

In autumn 2006, Gazprom announced that, contrary to previous expec-tations, it would develop the vast Shtokman field in the Barents Sea by itself, relying on foreign companies only as subcontractors rather than as shareholders. Foreign companies had been hoping to have as much as 49% of the shares.[48] Then, in July 2007, Gazprom, in an apparent reversal of this decision, signed an agreement giving the French company Total a 25% stake in the Shtokman field, while holding out the possibility of selling a further 24% stake to another foreign investor, thus putting the poten-tial foreign share of the project at 49%.[49] This dramatic about-turn on the part of the Russian energy giant may indicate a growing recognition on Moscow's part that foreign investors will indeed need to be brought in if the ambitious goal of keeping Russia as an 'energy superpower' is to be achieved. However, it also underscores the volatile nature of the country's investment climate.

The outward investment trend

In the meantime, Russian investors seem to be looking elsewhere for places to send their capital. As Putin noted with pride at the St Petersburg Economic Forum, in mid 2007, total Russian investment abroad amounted to at least $140bn.[50] Russia, Putin added, is 'interested in further expansion of Russian investment abroad, as well as [share swaps] on mutually advantageous terms with foreign partners'.[51]

Thus, what only a few years ago was considered to be a major problem for the country's economy – capital flight – is now viewed by the country's leadership as a sign of Russian international economic standing, and a tendency to be encouraged. The indignation among Russian politicians and commentators over the failure by a Russian steel tycoon to take over the Luxembourg steelmaker Arcelor in 2006 on the grounds that it showed Russophobia on the part of European businessmen and politicians was surely a sign of how much successfully taking Russian money abroad has become a matter of national pride in recent years.[52] But while the appeal of investing capital abroad is easy to understand, as it gives Russia added international prestige and leverage, such activity carries with it substantial costs, since the domestic demand for investment is clearly far from satisfied. Continued lack of investment in critical sectors such as energy could threaten to undermine Russia's fragile domestic equilibrium, and undermine its international aspirations, which are after all so closely linked to its claim to be an 'energy superpower'.

A precarious future?

In the long run, Russia's position in the international energy marketplace appears not to be as secure as its leaders might hope. The country's ability to sustain production is being openly questioned by increasing numbers of domestic and foreign experts. Russia has neither joined OPEC nor established itself as an influential independent player on the international oil market, and remains a price-taker, rather than a price-maker, largely at the mercy of consumers and other oil exporters. Its ambitions to organise a gas cartel – a 'gas OPEC' – are unlikely to be realised soon, because of its limited leverage vis-à-vis other gas producers; the inherent difficulty of organising and enforcing cartel arrangements among producers competing for the same markets; and the trend toward liberalisation of the gas market that is liable to undercut cartel power.

Russia's occasional bursts of enthusiasm for the idea of reorienting its gas exports from Europe to Asia run into the harsh reality of the difficulty of building major pipelines across Siberia and the geopolitical uncertainty of the relationship with China. The country's position as an 'energy super-power' is in practice largely limited to the former Soviet regions, where it plays a major role in any case, mostly for historical reasons. And even in the former Soviet Union, Russian energy policy is not absolute, as other energy producers – most notably Kazakhstan and Azerbaijan – have successfully pursued skilful strategies to gain the support of other major powers, including the US and China, for independent energy policies, and have developed their export options beyond Russia.

In sum, in spite of its unquestionable economic transformation, in the long run, Russia's claim to sustainable economic recovery, its aspirations to superpowerdom, energy or otherwise, and its place alongside the major economic powers all rest on uncertain foundations.

CHAPTER FIVE

The Military Factor

In an earlier era, few explorations of Russian foreign policy and its drivers would have left the discussion of the military's role in shaping and implementing this policy until close to the end of the discussion. For most of the post-Second World War era, Moscow's military capability was the prime instrument of its foreign policy, while the military institution itself reportedly played an important role in setting the country's international agenda. But in Putin's Russia, the former is evidently not the case. As to the latter, changes here are more difficult to determine: the policymaking process in modern-day Russia is not transparent to outsiders, and the task of calculating the correlation of forces in policy debates between various personalities and institutions is a large and complex one, that cannot be properly discharged here. Nevertheless, it would not be rash to state that the military establishment no longer sits as near the head of the table in policy debates as it did 20 years ago.[1]

The Russian military today

The format of this study precludes a detailed examination of the Russian military; instead this section will provide a general overview of the institution insofar as it relates to Russia's international position and foreign policy direction. In its present condition, the Russian military is certainly a long way from the zenith of power and prestige at home and abroad that the Soviet military achieved in the early 1980s.[2] At the same time, the Russian military of 2007 is also indisputably far from the nadir of its power and domestic and international standing that it reached in the mid 1990s.[3] It is difficult to predict with confidence whether in the coming years it will progress or fall back from the point at which it stands today.

The profound setbacks suffered by the military at the end of the Soviet era and the chaotic conditions in which it found itself after the break-up of the Soviet Union are amply documented.[4] Reports of soldiers going hungry, begging for money, bread or cigarettes in the streets of Moscow and at checkpoints in Chechnya, of officers who had not been paid for months living with their families in tents or dormitories without basic necessities, abounded in the Russian and foreign press in the 1990s. The Russian army seemed to be on the verge of disintegration.

This is no longer the case. The Russian military has come a long way since those dark days. It also has, for the moment at least, less to contend with in terms of major, live conflicts. The country's most acute security problem during the 1990s – the war in Chechnya – has been won, reduced to a low-level insurgency at most, with the help of persistent efforts on the part of the Kremlin to install a Chechen leadership capable of maintaining peace and relative security in the province. The methods of the chosen leadership are the subject of widespread criticism, while its prospects and longevity are the subject of equally widespread doubts. Nonetheless, the military campaign in Chechnya appears to be over.

Russian military budgets have been rising in line with the country's overall financial upturn. According to the IISS *Military Balance 2006*, the official 2006 defence budget was 666bn roubles (approximately $25bn) – a 25% increase from 2005 and twice what it was in 2003, though in real terms the increase over 2003 was 25%. Defence spending for 2007 is reportedly set at 860bn roubles.[5]

How and indeed whether the official figures correspond to actual spending could be the subject of a separate study. Nevertheless, there is no reason to doubt that budgets have been going up, and that the Russian military has had more resources at its disposal in the past eight years than it had during the 1990s.[6] However the extent to which it has reformed and modernised, and the degree to which this increased spending has translated into improved capabilities, remain subjects of some disagreement among both foreign and Russian analysts.

Numerically, the Russian military under the jurisdiction of the ministry of defence is a fraction of the size of its Soviet predecessor. According to *The Military Balance,* in 2006, the active duty strength of the Russian military was just over one million,[7] roughly a quarter of the size of the Soviet military at the end of the Cold War. Following several years of reductions and reorganisation, the military currently consists of three services: the army (360,000 men), navy (142,000 men) and air force (160,000 men), and three further branches – Strategic Rocket Forces (SRF) (40,000 men), Space Forces (40,000 men) and Airborne Troops (35,000 men).[8] In addition, the armed forces include Rear, Support and Railway Troops, as well as uniformed personnel who are not part of the ministry of defence.[9]

The nuclear deterrent

Despite deep cuts in its nuclear arsenal in line with US–Russian arms-control agreements, Russia still maintains a robust deterrent force. Its nearly 500 land-based, silo-based and mobile missiles can deliver nearly 1,800 warheads. Its 12 ballistic missile submarines carry more than 600 nuclear warheads. It also maintains nearly 80 bombers that can carry nearly 900 long-range nuclear-armed cruise missiles.[10]

The state of Russian nuclear forces and their future prospects have been the subject of particular scrutiny and controversy ever since the publication of a contentious *Foreign Affairs* article in 2006 that argued that the poor condition of Russian forces and contrasting US advances meant that the US was or would soon be in a position to be able to carry out a counterforce strike against Russia with impunity.[11] The article, cited earlier in this study in the context of a discussion of Russian concerns about US missile defence projects, triggered a series of vigorous Russian denials. Its argument is dubious, derived as it is from abstract calculations of nuclear exchanges, rather than the real world of practical policy. According to independent expert opinion, rumours of Russian nuclear forces' imminent demise are in any case greatly exaggerated.[12] No future Russian leadership is likely to allow the country's ultimate deterrent to atrophy. Equally, it is just as implausible that any future US leadership would launch a nuclear strike against Russia or exploit its vulnerability on the basis of abstract calculations of strategic imbalance and the prospects for such a strike's success.

Implicit comparisons of Russia's contemporary nuclear arsenal with that of the Soviet Union of the kind that was made in the article are inherently misleading, because Soviet arsenals were designed for fundamentally different purposes. Russia and the US are no longer locked in a nuclear stand-off. The notion that Russia needs capabilities for counterforce targeting against the United States is an obsolete one. Instead, the utility of its nuclear forces to Russia is, as we have seen, as a deterrent against both nuclear and conventional threats, and a guarantor of its strategic independence and sovereignty. Russia has in effect adopted a posture of minimal deterrence, whereby it maintains a relatively small nuclear arsenal, but one that is sufficiently robust to convince potential attackers that they would not be able to carry out a disarming strike against Russia, or threaten it or its interests conventionally.

While anachronistic comparisons of US and Russian capabilities may have little relevance to current realities, as we saw earlier, the effect that future American missile defences might potentially have on this minimal deterrent *is* a valid cause for anxiety as far as Russian military planners are concerned. In the abstract world of strategic nuclear exchange models, the United States' uncertain – and therefore from the Russian point of view, open-ended – plans for new BMD systems represent a worrying develop-ment. Hypothetically, in the worst-case scenario, from the Russian point of view, a future combination of US offensive capabilities and much-improved BMD could 'knock out' Russia's nuclear deterrent altogether.

Accordingly, current plans provide for a significant change in the mix of Russian land-based ballistic missiles. The ageing fixed, silo-based SS-18, SS-19 and SS-25 ICBMs are scheduled to be withdrawn from service by 2015.[13] Also by 2015, the SRF is to have 34 mobile and 66 silo-based SS-27 ICBMs.[14] With the expiry on 1 January 2009 of the ban on Multiple Independently Targeted Re-Entry Vehicles (MIRVs) imposed by the START I (first Strategic Arms Reduction Treaty), new missiles are reportedly planned to be fitted with MIRVed warheads,[15] which military planners hope will provide a sufficient hedge against future US BMD capabilities. At the end of this modernisation programme, the SRF is expected to have approximately 500 land-based warheads, and the total number of warheads, sea- and land-based, will be approximately 1,500; still well below the 2,200 limit set by the Moscow Treaty.[16]

In keeping with the minimal deterrent posture, the Russian ballistic missile submarine (SSBN) fleet is in the process of downsizing and, appar-ently, consolidating. Current estimates of the size of the Russian SSBN fleet vary, but the 2006 *Military Balance* puts it at 15 vessels. Another authorita-tive source has 13, of which six are *Delta III* submarines assigned to the Pacific Fleet; six are *Delta IVs* assigned to the Northern Fleet, and one is a *Typhoon* submarine, also with the Northern Fleet.[17] The entire *Delta III* class of submarines is reportedly planned to be withdrawn from service over the next few years,[18] and the navy reportedly plans to consolidate all SSBNs in the Northern Fleet.[19]

New vessels are coming online: the newest Russian *Borey*-class SSBN was reported to have been launched in April 2007 and to be expected to begin sea trials in October 2007. Two more submarines of the same class are also reported to be under construction.[20] Progress has been slow, however. Construction of this vessel began in 1996, and the April launch was, it now appears, 'symbolic', in the dry dock only, and further delays are expected.[21]

The programme of SSBN modernisation has been the target of severe criticism in the Russian media, and the plan to concentrate all SSBNs in the Northern Fleet is likely to run into internal opposition within the fleet, as a decision of such magnitude would be apt to do in any country. The programme has been hampered by numerous delays, and suffers from the effects of chronic underfunding.[22] Some critics of the programme contend that long-term underfunding and a lack of orders have done irreparable damage to the Russian ship-building industry, meaning that the industry will not have the capacity to fulfil the programme's requirements and sustain the projected rate of refitting and replacement.[23]

Nevertheless, despite powerful criticisms of the programme, existing and predicted setbacks, though severe, are not unique in the context of the development and fielding of major weapons systems, and there is little doubt that it is well within Russia's capabilities to maintain a credible deterrent at sea, as on land and in the air, in keeping with its minimal deterrence posture. When considering the attainability of Russia's ambitions in this field, it is worth remembering that only a relatively small number of weapons are after all needed in order for a minimal deterrent to be in place.

Military reform and modernisation

The conventional elements of Russian defence capabilities are subject to many of the same kinds of problems and uncertainties as faced by the country's nuclear capabilities, though in view of the special significance of the nuclear deterrent, the ill-effects of the previous decade are bound to linger longer in the conventional sphere. Years of underfunding and neglect, delayed modernisation, large-scale reductions in force sizes and unsuccessful attempts at reform have taken their toll on the Russian army, navy and air force.

Military reform, identified by Putin at the outset of his presidency as a matter of national priority, has been the subject of much controversy within Russia and among foreign observers for some time. A number of objectives have been pursued: various modes of redeployment in accordance with new challenges and domestic conditions, downsizing, restructuring and professionalisation. In 2003, Sergei Ivanov, then Putin's defence minister, famously declared the reform process, which might have been expected to be long and complex, to be completed.[24]

The downsizing aspect of the process had indeed been achieved in great part by that point, in crude terms of numerical cuts. The situation with other key aspects of reform was quite different, however, and the notion that the job was finished has since apparently been jettisoned: Ivanov subsequently announced plans for further reductions and restructurings on more than one occasion.[25] In January 2007, Chief of the General Staff General Yury Baluyevsky declared that 'the military reform is continuing' and would last 'indefinitely' because of new threats and a 'changed system of international relations'[26] (a clear reference to Russian concerns over NATO expansion and US involvement in the countries of the former Soviet Union).

Clearly, the reform is indeed a slow process. Regardless of its planned direction, it appears unlikely that it will have a major effect on Russia's defence capabilities or posture any time soon. This is due to the substantial systemic constraints with which the Russian military will have to contend for the foreseeable future, most crucially the size of the defence budget, the condition of the defence industries and the national demographic crisis.

Russia's demographic crisis, currently forecast to last indefinitely, is a major constraint on the size of the country's armed forces. As the military currently relies largely on conscripts to fill its ranks, it is already faced with a pool of manpower that fails to meet its requirements in terms of numbers and quality of recruits. Widespread poor health renders many Russian young men unfit for service, and poor pay and living conditions and chronic discipline problems, including the brutal victimisation of new recruits, lead many eligible men to seek deferments and exemptions by all possible means, leaving only a fraction of the conscript pool left for the military to pick from, which shrinks every year due to the low birth rates.[27]

The Russian military has been trying for some time to initiate a shift from an all-conscript army to a professional one. This effort has run into severe obstacles. Throughout the 1990s, when the national economy and military finances were in freefall, the professional military option was simply not viable, as the military had no means to pay professional soldiers. Once the economy recovered, the demographic problem that plagues the conscription process was soon found to similarly limit the availability of potential professional recruits. Even leaving aside the general unpopularity of military service, the armed forces are having to compete with the rest of the economy for a shrinking supply of labour.

There is particular demand for professional, non-conscripted soldiers to work in branches that require specialised technical skills, as well as in elite units such as the Airborne Troops, and this demand further diminishes the number of professional, or 'contract', soldiers available for service in the regular army. [28] This is likely to have an adverse ripple effect throughout the military, from overall levels of professional competence and readiness, to prospects for modernisation and upgrading of weapons and equipment, as certain skill levels are required to man and maintain sophisticated hardware.

The state of the defence industry and tight procurement budgets hold out pretty bleak prospects for modernisation in any case. Procurement budgets have been notoriously low for a long time, leaving the defence–industrial complex at the mercy of foreign buyers.[29] There has been some amelioration in recent years: budgets have risen, and funds for procurement, repairs and modernisation of old equipment, and research and development, increased to $11.6bn in 2007 – a 28% gain on 2006.[30] Official statements made in 2007 also point to a surge in spending in the period 2008 to 2010 as part of attempts to accelerate modernisation and reform.

However, despite a steady increase over several years, the numbers are still very modest, considering the size of the Russian military and the starvation diet that it and the defence industry have been on for so many years. The ministry of defence's shopping list for 2007 reportedly includes expensive high-priority items such as *Topol-M* ICBMs, *Sineva* submarine-launched ballistic missiles and *GLONASS-M* satellites for the Space Forces, as well as repairs and modernisation of the only remaining Russian aircraft carrier. The sums left over for upgrading the armed forces' conventional capabilities after these acquisitions and improvements are not likely to be great.[31]

In the virtually unanimous opinion of Russian experts, the Russian defence industry is struggling to overcome the ill-effects of the 1990s – poor quality and high unit costs due to outdated equipment and limited production runs. While the Russian military may now have more money to spend on what the Russian defence industry has to offer, defeating the legacy of neglect of those years is a task that the industry is by no means guaranteed to accomplish.[32]

Prospects

If measured by the Cold War-era correlation of forces yardstick, the military balance is not in Russia's favour in the west (NATO), the east (China) or the south (unstable regions and borders, and China). This outlook is reflected in the 2003 doctrine-like document 'Current Tasks of Development of the Armed Forces',[33] which includes a map of threats to Russian security that would have seemed a nightmarish vision to a chief of the general staff from the Soviet era such as Marshal Ogarkov. Ogarkov, a noted writer on the radical impact of technological change on warfare, the 'revolution in military affairs', would have seen a Russia left behind by that 'revolution', and facing threats to its security directly on its borders, both from NATO and from weak states, transnational agents and nuclear proliferation.

However, Russian security is no longer measured by Cold War yard-sticks. And although Russia lacks the sophisticated weaponry fielded by some of its NATO partners/potential adversaries, and Russian military planners may tend to focus on worst-case scenarios and insist that it is the capability that counts, it is difficult to imagine circumstances in which this capabilities gap would become relevant.

Russia, despite the profound problems that its military has experienced over the past decade-and-a-half, and which still severely hamper it, remains the biggest, even, arguably, the only credible military presence in the space of the former Soviet Union, and, in spite of the severe shortfalls detailed above, it nevertheless has and is acquiring capabilities that are likely to be relevant to the kinds of challenges it and its neighbours could face in that giant region in the foreseeable future.

In the security environment that is likely to develop over the coming years, it seems improbable that Russia would need the kinds of advanced conventional capabilities that Marshal Ogarkov envisaged nearly a generation ago as essential for a modern military institution. The fact that Russia has not gone through the revolution in military affairs is likely to turn out to be largely irrelevant to its ability to project power in support of its political objectives or intervene in crises on its periphery. Its nuclear deterrent is performing the critical mission of deterring the 'big war'. Its conventional capabilities, relatively low-tech as they might be by the standards of the twenty-first century, appear nevertheless to be adequate to their current and likely future tasks – counter-insurgency operations in the North Caucasus; stability operations and crisis interventions in the neighbouring countries; peacekeeping missions and 'showing the flag', most likely either in the ex-Soviet region, or in UN-mandated situations.

The infusion of cash into the military that has accompanied the country's financial revival, although not substantial by modern standards, and not always well spent, is very gradually making it possible for the military to boost its conventional capabilities and improve their quality, professionalism and combat readiness, though, as we have seen, it is a slow and difficult journey, with many obstacles in the way. Renewed spending has been accompanied by a willingness on the part of the military establishment to reorient its improving capabilities towards more realistic missions on Russia's periphery, as opposed to far-fetched scenarios of large-scale conflict with NATO.

The spectre of a large-scale conventional war will undoubtedly remain in Russian military minds, and on the list of possible contingencies. However, for it to be taken seriously by Russian military planners as a priority threat would require such a radical reversal of Russia's political fortunes that for the foreseeable future they show no signs of allowing it to significantly affect their planning and posture. In practice, the real-time deployable capabilities of the Russian military are most likely to be concentrated in the near future in elite components such as the Airborne Troops, select ground-troop units and Special Forces, including some belonging to agencies other than the ministry of defence.[34]

All the same Russia, in perceiving itself as a gravitational pole of the multipolar world, will, unlike any other former Soviet or Warsaw Pact state, not be content to have military institutions suitable only as providers of niche capabilities to the international military operations of organisations like NATO. For a country of Russia's size and military tradition, no amount of rational estimation of probable need can overcome the cultural demand for the maintenance of a large military establishment. Russia's million-strong force is psychologically an important asset, in addition to being a basic mobilisational framework for responding to a major contingency.

There are traumas to be overcome as the military adapts itself in the coming years. Its performance in Chechnya has been the subject of widespread criticism both inside and outside Russia. The memory of humiliating defeats inflicted on Russian armed forces by a small but skilled and dedicated opponent is unlikely to fade soon. The Chechen experience is particularly sensitive because, unlike in Afghanistan, the war in Chechnya was a conflict in which the Russian army's enemy did not have the benefit of vast amounts of foreign material support and technical assistance. But assuming that the necessary will and vision are there to put it to use, Chechnya could also be valuable to the Russian military, as direct relevant experience on which to draw when shaping the battlefield doctrine and developing capabilities to meet future challenges to Russian security.

The future of the Russian military is not by any means clear. It is neither the spent force that it was in the 1990s, nor the mighty military machine that a simple reading of the numbers involved might lead one to imagine. Though a legacy of neglect, poor demographics and comparative underfunding are serious handicaps, in areas where key Russian interests are concentrated, the Russian military has re-emerged as a presence to be reckoned with. Moreover, it is in a position, as long as the right decisions are made, to continue along this evolutionary path and remain a military power second to none throughout the territories of the former Soviet Union.

CONCLUSION

Russia is once again an important actor on the world stage. It is a country with considerable means at its disposal, which, its leaders hope, will enable it to play a major part in world affairs appropriate to its size, resources and history. Accordingly, an expansive vision has so far guided Russia's return to the international arena. However, at the moment, as we have seen, the country's ambitious vision exceeds the resources available to it. Moreover, in the course of making itself heard in the international arena, Russia has succeeded in frightening many, while reassuring and winning over very few, if any, thus raising further questions about the long-term sustainability of its posture.

Domestic support for Putin's foreign policy and his personal popularity (which, as we have seen, owes a good deal to his foreign policy stance), should not be interpreted as evidence of a stable equilibrium in Russian politics. Russia still is a country where many fundamental questions remain unanswered, where major new political forces are taking shape, and where debates about the country's direction are at a very early stage. In other words, it is a country where in the long run domestic political stability is far from guaranteed.

Equally, Russia's economic recovery, while impressive, is no guarantee of sustained growth and economic development. The dire decade of the 1990s may seem to be a distant memory, but the recovery has been uneven, and driven to a great extent by high energy prices. The jury is still out on whether the country is making use of its newfound wealth in a way that will enable it to restructure its economy and lay the foundations for sustained growth, though as we have seen, current signs are not encouraging. Furthermore, in view of the state of current reserves and the uncertain outlook for mobilising the necessary investment to tap and exploit new deposits, Russia's future as an 'energy superpower' is in doubt.

Militarily, Russia appears to be well past the worst. The military has been receiving more resources year after year, downsizing and reconstituting its capabilities. The result has been a smaller, but qualitatively improved force, better suited to handling key challenges to Russian security than at any time since the break-up of the Soviet Union. The Russian military is again a considerable presence in the territory of the former Soviet Union, the region that matters to it the most. However, it is still short on power-projection capabilities and faces major obstacles on the way to its apparent goal of re-establishing itself as the security arbiter in the former Soviet lands.

Russia's ability to synchronise its projected vision of itself with the means at its disposal will be crucial to its success in the international arena. On this assessment of the domestic political, economic and military foundations of Russian foreign policy, there is much work to be done.

Changes abroad

For some time, Russian elites and the general public seemed content to coast along on the back of Russia's newfound prosperity, stability and international recognition. But Russia risks falling victim to stagnation at home and being left unprepared for new challenges abroad. Changes are taking place on Russia's doorstep that the country seems to be ill-equipped to handle. In the radically altered geopolitical landscape of Eurasia, new superpower actors include China, India and Europe, all of which show signs of much greater economic dynamism, activity on the foreign policy front and – before long – military capability than Russia. Moscow is already having to contend with these new powers in Eurasian geopolitics while it tries to reassert itself in its own neighbourhood. Its ability to compete against these actors for market share, political influence and access to resources is very much in doubt.

There is also the challenge of a post-Iraq War Middle East, where Iran, Russia's principal partner, is proving increasingly difficult to handle, and where change could be rapid, unpredictable and close to Russian borders. Turkey is undergoing its own strategic transition and redefining its role in Europe and in the Middle East, and its re-evaluation of its strategic circumstances is likely to have far-reaching implications for Russia. Lastly, and importantly, there is the necessity of forging a new relationship with the United States, as, post-Iraq, it rethinks its role in the world and attempts to redefine its key relationships.

Russia's sovereignty itself is looking increasingly challenged, especially if viewed in the terms of the Putin government, as freedom from external sources of influence. Regained through economic revival and political stability, Russian sovereignty rests on the foundation of oil and gas. In addition to the vulnerability of any country overly reliant for its economic wellbeing on exports of commodities and minerals, Russia, outside OPEC, and with little prospect of succeeding in forming the gas cartel it has mooted in the past, also suffers from a relatively weak position in the global oil market.

Policy adjustments

The task of recalibrating Russia's foreign-policy vision in order to address these issues is a delicate one for Russia's leaders. An overly modest vision is unlikely to gain the necessary support of the Russian political class or the public. A vision that is too ambitious promises risks for which few in Russia have an appetite, including the risk of over-extension, which would trigger traumatic memories, never far from Russian minds, of the Soviet decline.

Given the relatively weak domestic political impetus for alteration of Russian foreign policy, the speed at which adjustment will occur will depend on the country's ability to sustain its economic performance, and on the pace of change in the international environment. At the moment any substantial reassessment of Russia's international outlook appears to be a mid-term – five to 10 years – rather than a short-term prospect.

In the course of this revision, Russian leaders will need to ask themselves whether their country's prospects for playing a key role in the international arena are enhanced or constrained by their partnership with the West. They will also need to consider whether the present course, which sees Russia often walking alone, and which so far has created no durable alliances for Russia, but rather has alienated a number of potential partners, is sustainable for a country that aspires to be a world leader.

At the point at which such decisions might be made, Russia is likely to be presented with two choices: a junior partnership with China; or a renewed partnership with the West. The latter will probably appear more attractive to Russian leaders and citizens, given their long-standing apprehensions about China. However, in order to be more fruitful than earlier overtures, the next Russian attempt to forge a partnership with the West will need to address the question of common values, so important to the West, but, it would seem, not so important to Russia. This adjustment will be crucial to the success of any effort towards westward integration.

The view from the West

A realistic policy for the US and its European allies to adopt towards Russia will hinge on an equally realistic assessment of what Russia is. Understanding its internal conditions, its capabilities and its motivations in the international arena, as well as the conditions and behaviour of its neighbours, is an essential precondition of a successful approach to Russia and the vast region that surrounds it. Inflated assessments of Russia's impact on the region could prove just as harmful as underestimating its importance.

The West and Russia are not, despite widespread apprehensions, heading into a new cold war. However, a period of adjustment in the relationship is long overdue, and dealing with Russia in the years to come should and will be an important top-tier task for Western leaders and their foreign-policy teams. Neglect here is fraught with long-term negative consequences for all involved.

Russia's 'near abroad'

The issue of Russia's domineering presence in its neighbourhood is perhaps the single most troubling issue affecting the West's overall relationship with Russia. How might the US and Europe best approach this challenge in which geopolitics and values intersect?

As we have seen, the ex-Soviet and Warsaw Pact lands, Russia's 'near abroad', remain the region of primary strategic concern for Moscow. Russia's insistence that it has special interests and responsibilities in these vast territories has led it to behave in ways that the West has strongly opposed.

Some in the West have worried that Russian foreign policy in this sphere is neo-imperialist, designed to restore by bullying and stealth to Russia what it lost in the break-up of the Soviet Union. But, the overweening quality of much of Russia's policy towards its neighbours notwithstanding, it is surely wiser to view the current Russian approach rather as post-imperial, part of a process of adjustment as Russia and its neighbours work out ways of dealing with each other in the post-Soviet era. A post-imperial policy, while tinged with nostalgia for the old regime and its possessions, is essentially one of adaptation to a new and greatly diminished condition.[1]

It is important to remember that Russia has accepted, albeit grudgingly, two rounds of NATO enlargement, one round of EU enlargement, US and other NATO countries' deployments to Central Asia and active security relationships with Ukraine, Georgia and other former Soviet states. Moscow is becoming aware that throughout the near abroad, it must find ways of successfully competing for market access and political influence with Europe, the US and China. It may not be glad to see these vast and rapid changes in its neighbourhood, but it does not deny them.

It is also possible to see Moscow's record on relations with its neighbours in a more favourable light than the condemnatory one in which it is usually viewed. Aggressive behaviour during Ukraine's 'Orange Revolution' and the imposition of sanctions on Georgia notwithstanding, Moscow has also acted with implicit recognition of its own limitations in its region, and backed away when met with a firm and clear response, especially when that response has had the support of the United States and Europe, as for example during the Estonia crisis.

As regards Moscow's use of energy trade for political gains, it is arguably Moscow's prerogative to deny favourable terms to neighbouring states which try to pursue foreign policies unfavourable to Russian interests. If Ukraine or Georgia wants to pursue membership in NATO or the EU against Moscow's wishes, it is perhaps only fair that Moscow cease subsidising it with cheap Russian gas.

Russia's heavy-handed policies toward its neighbours have prompted a natural tendency on the part of Europe and the US to side with the victims of these policies, and criticise Russia for enacting them. But a desire to support the underdog should not lead the West to turn a blind eye to the fact that while such policies may be undesirable, the difficult circumstances in which some of Russia's neighbours have found themselves are not all of Russia's making. For instance, despite repeated Russian attempts to intervene in Ukrainian politics following the 'Orange Revolution', the succession of political crises that have erupted in the years since then appears to be the result of profound divisions in Ukrainian domestic politics rather than the product of Russian interference. Similarly, though Russia's policies towards Georgia have indisputably done lasting harm to Georgia and Georgian–Russian relations, many of Georgia's internal troubles derive from indigenous political, ethnic and regional tensions going back to the early period of Georgian independence, the rule of its first elected president, Zviad Gamsakhurdia, and the catastrophic civil war.

Russia's behaviour can make it easy to blame Russia for its neighbours' troubles and look for solutions to their problems in Moscow. But more lasting solutions can perhaps be found within these nations' own boundaries. For example, rather than castigating Russia for raising the price of the gas it sells to Ukraine, a long-term solution might be reached by helping Ukraine to achieve energy independence through a sensible energy policy – something that Ukrainian governments have been unwilling or unable to do for a long time, regardless of Moscow's actions.

Of course, if the consolidation and expansion of its sphere of influence is Moscow's objective, then its current approach has proven singularly unsuccessful, but it is not in an easy position, and careful differentiation between specific situations and a subtlety of approach will be essential for Western policies towards Moscow to succeed in this area.

Economics

In the sphere of trade and economic relations, close scrutiny and regulation of and the imposition of limits on Russian investment projects abroad should not be criticised as protectionism. Leading Russian companies pursuing foreign investment opportunities, such as Gazprom for example, are majority-owned by the Russian state, have close ties to the Kremlin and have senior government officials serving on or chairing their boards. The Russian government's insistence on exerting tight control over strategic sectors of the country's economy is understandable, and this can and should be reciprocated by the West.

The gas trade between Russia and Europe is a relationship of mutual dependence. As we have seen, Europe is dependent on Russia for nearly a quarter of its natural gas, which in turn meets nearly a quarter of its overall energy demand. Though Russia in return depends on Europe for a market for its gas, Europe needs all the same to diversify its energy supplies in order to limit its dependence on Russia, and, even more importantly, it needs to develop a common energy strategy to counter Russian leverage in this sphere. Advances in liquefied natural gas (LNG) technology hold out the promise of liberalising the gas market and reducing Europe's pipeline dependency. The technology and infrastructure are not yet advanced enough for this to be a viable option for the short term, but in the long run LNG could offer Europe increased leverage with Russia.

Democratisation

Western opportunities for influencing Russian domestic and foreign behaviour are relatively few. Aid is no longer needed or welcome in a country now awash with money. Technical assistance is hardly in demand either, as, after a decade-and-a-half of exposure to Western expertise, Russia has developed its own technical competence and expertise in key areas. Democracy promotion is not welcome, nor is it helpful, in the words of George F. Kennan, to 'hover nervously, applying litmus papers daily to their political complexions to find out whether they answer to our concept of "democratic"'. Better instead to 'Give them time; let them be Russians; let them work out their internal problems in their own manner.'[2]

One of the pivotal questions facing the United States and Europe in their dealings with Russia is nevertheless the issue of Russian domestic arrangements, and whether and how the West should involve itself in Russia's internal affairs. At the risk of edging towards prescription, so far avoided in this study, this writer believes that a democratic Russia would be in the West's interest. It appears that many, though not all, current disagreements between Russia and the West derive from differing values, rather than conflicting interests. Thus it is reasonable to assume that a foundation of shared democratic values and a commitment to shared principles would enable Russia and the West to develop a far more constructive relationship than the one they have managed to achieve so far. When considering how such a common foundation might be built, a few points should be borne in mind.

Firstly, this will need to be a two-way process, requiring adaptation on the part of the West as well as Russia. This does not mean compromising on principle, but it does mean that Russian concerns need to be heard by the West, rather than simply dismissed, as has been the case on occasion over the past decade-and-a-half, and at times accommodations may need to be made. It is important to recognise that the West is no longer the mentor, and Russia no longer the student.

Secondly, in the past, inflated expectations have led to disappointment and a sense of betrayal on both sides. Perhaps the most important lesson for Western policy on Russian domestic affairs is the necessity of taking the long view, of fully internalising the idea that change in Russia will take generations. Patience is paramount. It would help, too, to avoid terms like 'strategic partnership' and 'alliance' when describing relations with Russia, even if the relationship takes a turn for the better in the years to come.

Thirdly, the US and Europe should target resources where they are needed, and solicit input from Russians themselves, not just from Western analysts, in this regard. Few Western initiatives have elicited as much scorn from Russians as US and European attempts to promote democracy in Russia, which are viewed as either naive or subversive. This is an issue that needs to be handled with utmost care, keeping in mind the uninspiring record of Western-sponsored democracy promotion in Russia in the 1990s.

The West's toolkit for helping Russia to move towards democracy is limited. Russia can be neither coerced nor enticed into democracy. The West has too few carrots and sticks to be able to apply meaningful pressure or offer significant rewards to such a vast and diverse nation. But to say that the West has few levers for influencing Russian behaviour at home and abroad is not the same thing as saying it is powerless to do anything. Some powerful levers are available. Efforts on the part of Americans and Europeans to engage, explain, listen and watch carefully, and help wherever help is sought and possible to give, will be important to the process of drawing Russia closer. By contrast, narrow and directive approaches, such as teaching Russians how to organise political parties and monitor elections, are unlikely to prove meaningful or useful.

Western efforts should be targeted in a number of important areas specifically:

- The provision of free, unbiased and comprehensive information to Russians about Russia and the world; this can be achieved via the Internet, web-based television programming or radio
- The expansion of opportunities for Russian students to attend Western universities on either a long- or short-term basis
- The expansion of opportunities for Western and Russian academics to teach at each other's universities and boost their professional contacts
- The engagement of the Russian strategic community in dialogue about current and future challenges facing Russia, the US and Europe
- Making available senior American and European officials and prominent non-governmental experts in various fields to address Russian audiences on the subject of major intellectual and political currents in the US, Europe and elsewhere, and other efforts to engage Russian audiences in a 'dialogue of civilisations' across a wide range of issues

It is important to cast these measures to audiences in both Russia and the West not as assistance to Russia, but as an investment in the relationship. It is equally important to treat this as a matter of enlightened self-interest on the part of Western powers, without unrealistic expectations, or goals of near-term or even eventual pay-offs in mind. This investment in relations with Russia may after all have to be made at a time when relations with Russia are tenser than they will have been for some time.

Diplomacy

At the formal diplomatic level, resolve is crucial. If the US and each of the countries of Europe fail to speak with one voice to Russia and present a single position on important matters, then it is pointless, as well as counter-productive, to accuse Russia of attempting to undermine Western solidarity. The Russian practice of exploiting transatlantic differences has a long history and is easy to recognise, and it has a powerful antidote in the form of transatlantic solidarity. Russian moves aimed at splitting Europe from the US (such as threats to the Czechs and Poles over US BMD installations, sweetener offers of energy deals to various European countries, intimidatory sabre-rattling at European neighbours) have so far mostly backfired, but it is important that they are not allowed to succeed in the future. Russia, if faced with a firm transatlantic position, will have to consider the possibility of being isolated from the circles in which it is seeking enhanced recognition and acceptance as an equal. This is a message that Russian audiences at every level need to hear with clarity and consistency. If Western governments and leaders want Russia to hear their messages of concern about its foreign policy or domestic affairs, candour and consistency in the relationship cannot be the preserve of lower-level officials, while summit proceedings remain full of bonhomie and good cheer.

It has become customary in recent years to state that the international community is better positioned to handle major challenges – Iranian and North Korean nuclear pursuits, troubles in the Middle East, weapons proliferation and terrorism – with Russia as a partner than without it. This is undeniably true. However, excessive enthusiasm for this view risks leading to the false impression that these problems cannot be tackled without Russia. In fact, as this discussion has demonstrated, Russian leverage in relation to most of these challenges is limited at best, and as and when viable responses to them are found, Russia's role is likely to be marginal – contributing its face to the image of solidarity in the international community, and lending the imprimatur of the UN Security Council.

Thus, while it is important to secure Russian participation in projects to resolve major international crises, it is just as important not to fall into the trap of making Russian participation a precondition for addressing such crises. This would make the issue of Russian participation into a roadblock and give Russia an effective veto on matters to which it has little to contribute. The West's solidarity and its willingness to act on issues that matter to it, with or without Russia, will be crucial to the success of any major diplomatic initiative.

The values gap

Western leaders are apt to forego the use of an important and potentially highly effective lever in their dealings with Russian counterparts. Not only does Russia seek acceptance and recognition in the councils of major – Western – powers, but Russians view themselves as Europeans and tend to have a sense of affinity with the West and many aspects of its culture. If Western leaders are sincere in their commitment to shared values, if the Western alliance has reached the point where its shared values in effect represent one of its chief interests, then they should benignly exploit this feeling and be publicly candid with Russia's leaders and its citizens that for as long as the values gap remains, Russia and its leaders will be viewed and treated as outsiders.

The West needs to be clear with Russian leaders that their acceptance of Russia is dependent on what Russia itself does. This point does not need to be framed as a take-it-or-leave-it proposition, and US and European leaders should signal and encourage open dialogue with their Russian counterparts and the Russian public. They should emphasise that the door to integration is wide open, and show a willingness to be open-minded and creative in defining Russia's place in this community. However, they should also be clear that acceptance of Russia will not be dictated by the state of Russian gas reserves, and that Russia cannot set the terms of its acceptance. A partnership, community, or some other form of association yet to be defined that is dependent on the reading on Russia's gas gauge is not in the interests of the West or Russia.

NOTES

Introduction

1   Thomas Graham, Jr, 'World Without Russia?', paper delivered at the Jamestown Foundation Conference, 9 June 1999, available at http://www.carnegieendowment.org/publications/index.cfm?fa=view&id=285.

2   *Ibid.*

3   The text of Putin's speech to the Munich Conference, 'Vystupleniya i Diskussiya na Myunkhenskoy Konferentsii po Voprosam Politiki Bezopasnosti', 10 February 2007, is available on the Kremlin website at http://www.kremlin.ru. See also Luke Harding, 'Russian Threatening New Cold War Over Missile Defence', *Guardian*, 11 April 2007, http://www.guardian.co.uk/frontpage/story/0,,2054144,00.html.

4   Alexander Timoshik, 'Russia to Target US Facilities in Poland and Czech Republic', *Pravda.ru*, 20 February 2007, http://english.pravda.ru/world/americas/20-02-2007/87573-Russia_target_Poland_Czech_Repu-0.

5   President Vladimir Putin, 'Interview Zhurnalistam Pechatnykh Sredstv Massovoy Informatsii iz Stran-Chlenov "Gruppy Vos'mi"', 4 June 2007, http://www.kremlin.ru.

6   'Vladimir Putin Podpisal Ukaz o Priostanovlenii Rossiyksoy Federatsiey Desystviya Dogovora ob Obychnykh Vooruzhennykh Silakh v Evrope i Svyazannykh s Nim Mezhdunarodnykh Dogovorov', http://www.kremlin.ru/text/news/2007/07/137831.shtml.

7   Putin, 'Vystupleniye na Voyennom Parade v Chest' 62-y Godovshchiny Pobedy v Velikoy Otechestvennoy Voyne', 9 May 2007, http://www.kremlin.ru.

Chapter One

1   For examples of work largely focused on Russia's domestic considerations in this period, see Peter Reddaway and Dmitri Glinski, *Tragedy of Russia's Reforms: Market Bolshevism Against Democracy* (Washington DC: United States Institute of Peace, 2001); Michael McFaul, *Russia's Unfinished Revolution: Political Change from Gorbachev to Putin* (Ithaca, NY: Cornell University Press, 2002); Anders Aslund, *How Russia Became a Market Economy*, (Washington DC: Brookings Institution Press, 1995).

2   Andrey Kozyrev, 'Russia: A Chance for Survival', *Foreign Affairs*, Spring 1992, p. 10.

3   *Ibid.*, p. 9.

4   See Francis Fukuyama, 'The End of History?', *The National Interest*, Summer 1989, http://www.marion.ohio-state.edu/fac/vsteffel/web597/Fukuyama_history.pdf; Robert B. Reich, *The Work of Nations: Preparing Ourselves for 21ˢᵗ Century Capitalism* (New York: Knopf, 1991); John Williamson, 'What Washington Means by Policy Reform', http://www.iie.com/publications/papers/print.cfm?doc=pub&ResearchID=486.

5   The most authoritative statement on this theme, which followed a protracted period during which foreign policy featured little in national debates in the US, is Henry Kissinger's 2001 book *Does America Need a Foreign Policy?* (New York: Simon and Schuster, 2001).

6   For a succinct and highly useful description see Thomas Carothers, 'The End of the Transition Paradigm', *Journal of Democracy*, vol. 13, no. 1, January 2002, pp. 5–21.

7   See Strobe Talbott, 'Gogol's Troika: The Case for Strategic Patience in a Time of Troubles', address to Stanford University, 6 November 1998, http://www.stanford.edu/group/Russia20/volumepdf/talbott.pdf.

8   President Bill Clinton, 'Remarks at the Signing Ceremony of NATO–Russia Founding Act', Paris, 27 May 1997, http://www.nato.int/docu/speech/1997/s970527d.htm.

9   Greg Craig and Ronald Asmus, 'The Rewards of a Larger NATO', *Washington Post*, 19 February 2007, http://www.washingtonpost.com/wp-dyn/content/article/2007/02/18/AR2007021800902.html.

10 Clinton, 'Remarks at the Signing Ceremony of NATO–Russia Founding Act'.

11 James Goldgeier and Michael McFaul, *Power and Purpose: American Policy Toward Russia After the Cold War* (Washington DC: Brookings Institution Press, 2003); interview with Madeleine Albright, NewsHour, Public Broadcasting Service (PBS), Arlington, VA, 14 May 1997, http://www.pbs.org/newshour/bb/international/jan-june97/albright_5-14.html.

12 'Foreign Investment Boom in Russia Persists', *Kommersant*, 22 May 2007, http://www.kommersant.com/p767358/Foreign_Investments_Statistics/.

13 One of the latest and most authoritative of such statements is to be found in 'Obzor Vneshney Politiki Rossiyskoy Federatsii' [Survey of the Foreign Policy of the Russian Federation], published by the Russian foreign ministry on 27 March 2007, http://www.ln.mid.ru/brp_4.nsf/sps/ 3647DA97748A106BC32572AB002AC4DD.

Chapter Two

1   Putin, 'Interview Zhurnalistam Pechatnykh Sredstv Massovoy Informatsii iz Stran-Chlenov "Gruppy Vos'mi"'.

2   *Ibid.*

3   Putin, 'Vystupleniye na Soveshchanii s Poslami i Postoyannymi Predstavitelyami Rossiyskoy Federatsii', 27 June 2006, http://www.kremlin.ru/appears/2006/06/27/1543_type63374type63377type63378type82634_107802.shtml.

4   *Ibid.*

5. *Ibid.*

6   The degree of self-worth and confidence reflected in this approach is all the more remarkable because it is in stark contrast to many statements delivered by Putin early in his presidency. In his first address to the nation, on 30 December 1999, made just before he took over from Yeltsin, Putin famously set the goal of catching up with

Portugal's or Spain's level of economic performance. There were even passages in his speech reminiscent of Kozyrev's 'normal' country: '[Russia] has entered the highway by which the whole of humanity is travelling. Only this way offers the possibility of dynamic economic growth and higher living standards, as world experience convincingly shows. There is no alternative to it.' At the top of Putin's international agenda at the end of 1999 was the task of making Russia attractive to foreign investors. Beyond this, his first address to the nation did not devote any time to foreign policy. Putin, 'Russia at the Turn of the Millenium', 30 December 1999, http://www.geocities.com/capitolhill/parliament/3005/poutine.html. Compare this vision of the path to be followed by Russia on the way to prosperity, not charted for itself, but by others, with Putin's speech at the International Economic Forum in St Petersburg in June 2007: 'I am convinced that general words about equitable distribution of resources and investment will resolve nothing. In the interest of sustainable development it is necessary to form a new architecture of mutually profitable international economic relations … International financial institutions need to be seriously restructured and modernised. They were designed for very different realities and cannot find their place in the conditions of sustained economic growth in most developing countries and growing markets. Thus, it is obvious that the world financial system tied to one or two currencies does not reflect the needs of the global economy. Fluctuations of these currencies negatively affect currency reserves of whole countries, the development of entire branches of the economy of the world as a whole. There is only one answer to this challenge: establishment of several global reserve currencies, several financial centres. That is why today it is necessary to create preconditions for diversification of reserves in the global financial system.' 'Stenograficheskiy Otchyot o Zasedanii XI Peterburgskogo Mezhdunarodnogo Ekonomicheskogo Foruma po Teme "Konkurentnosposobnaya Yevraziya – Prostranstvo Doveriya"', 10 June 2007, http://www.kremlin.ru. For more on this speech and what it says about Russia's international posture, see Chapter Four, pp. 56–7.

7   A prominent Russian parliamentarian declared boldly in the early 1990s that 'Russia's interests know no boundaries': Russia was more than what the Russian Federation within its post-1991 borders amounted to. Yevgeny Ambartsumov, 'Interesy Rossii ne Znayut Granits', *Megapolis Express*, 6 May 1992. Yeltsin also spoke about Russia's special role in the former Soviet lands, see Leslie H. Gelb, 'Yeltsin as a Monroe', *New York Times*, 7 March 1993. The idea that Russia would build a 'liberal empire' throughout the former Soviet lands was articulated in 2003 by leading Russian reformer of the 1990s Anatoly Chubais, see Igor Torbakov, 'Russian Policymakers Air Notion of "Liberal Empire" in Caucasus, Central Asia', Eurasia Insight, 27 October 2003, http://www.eurasianet.org/departments/insight/articles/eav102703.shtml. See also Torbakov, 'Russia Mulls Recognition of Independence for Georgian Separatist Regions', Eurasia Insight, 4 October 2004, http://www.eurasianet.org/departments/insight/articles/eav100404.shtml.

8   Dmitri Trenin, 'Russia and Central Asia', in *Central Asia: Views from Washington, Moscow and Beijing* (Armonk, NY and London: ME Sharpe, 2007), p. 81.

9   It should be noted that although disagreements over US plans for deploying missile defence components in Poland and the Czech Republic have emerged as a major stumbling block in US–Russian relations, Russia has also been engaged in discussions with NATO about European missile defence and Russian cooperation in it. These discussions have been relatively constructive and devoid of the heated rhetoric that has surrounded American deployment plans. Moreover,

NATO–Russia theatre missile defence cooperation is apparently aimed at deflecting some of the same threats targeted by the US-planned system, such as nuclear-armed rogue states. The author is grateful to IISS Senior Fellow Colonel (retd) Christopher Langton for bringing this important point to his attention. Information on NATO–Russia theatre missile defence cooperation is available on the NATO and NATO–Russia Council websites: http://www.nato-russia-council. info/HTM/EN/news_11.shtml; http:// www.nato.int/issues/missile_defence/ practice.html.

[10] Neil Buckley, 'Why the Kremlin is Making a Stand Over Missile Defence', FT.com, 7 June 2007, http://www. ft.com/cms/s/1aad9f8a-1525-11dc-b48a-000b5df10621,dwp_uuid=03d100e8-2fff-11da-ba9f-00000e2511c8,print=yes.html.

[11] Pavel Podvig, 'Missile Defense Interceptors in Poland', russianforces. org, 24 May 2006, http://russianforces. org/blog/2006/05/missile_defense_inter-ceptors_i.shtml; Stratfor, 'Russia, US: Putin Tells Bush Where to Put his Missile Defense System', 8 June 2007.

[12] Nikolay Ogarkov, *Vsegda v Gotovnosti k Zashchite Otechestva* (Moscow: Voyenizdat, 1982).

[13] Michael Fredholm, 'The Russian Energy Strategy and Energy Policy: Pipeline Diplomacy or Mutual Dependence?', Conflict Studies Research Centre, September 2005, http://66.102.9.104/sea rch?q=cache:4U5gWjqllxcJ:www.defac. ac.uk/colleges/csrc/document-listings/ russian/05(41)-MF.pdf+russia+vulnerable +pipeline&hl=en&ct=clnk&cd=9&gl=uk.

[14] See 'Vneshnepoliticheskiye Kontakty' [foreign policy contacts], http://www. kremlin.ru/sdocs/appears.shtml?day=& month=05&year=2007&prefix=%2Fincl udes%2Fappears%2F&value_from=%2 Fincludes%2Fappears%2F2007%2F05% 2F01&value_to=%2Fincludes%2Fappea rs%2F2007%2F05%2F31&date=05.2007 &type=63377&dayRequired=no&day_ enable=true&Submit.x=4&Submit.y=4;

Jean-Christophe Peuch, 'Russia: Energy Summit Gives Putin New Trump Card', Radio Free Europe/Radio Liberty, 16 May 2007, http://www.rferl.org/featuresarticle/ 2007/05/2c66d7b7-9c7e-465e-a263-11a3fbab043a.html; Breffni O'Rourke, 'Putin Visits Energy-Rich Kazakhstan, Turkmenistan', Radio Free Europe/Radio Liberty, 9 May 2007, http://www.rferl.org/ featuresarticle/2007/05/ed4dd349-0679-4844-80ec-cd246235f7ff.html.

[15] Stratfor, 'The Looming Central Asian Battleground', 20 August 2007; 'China: Central Asian Rumbles', 31 August 2007, [members' access only]; Radio Free Europe/Radio Liberty, 'Kazakhstan Proposes Caspian–Black Sea Canal', 10 June 2007, http://www.rferl.org/featuresarticle/ 2007/06/B8D010E3-CD3B-4CD9-976C-08B6F85D0BFE.html.

[16] 'Post-Soviet Space: A Disappearing Reality', chapter in *Mir Vokrug Rossii: 2017 Kontury Nedalekogo Budushchego* ['World Around Russia: 2017, the Contours of the Near Future'], (Moscow: Council for Foreign and Defence Policy, 2007), Polit. ru, 14 March 2007, http://www.polit. ru/research/2007/03/14/2017_print.html. See also http://www.svop.ru/upload/ images/2017_final.pdf for full text of book.

[17] *Ibid.*

[18] Aleksey Malashenko, 'Faktor Islama v Rossiyskoy Vneshney Politike', *Rossiya v Global'noy Politike*, no. 2, March–April 2007.

[19] *Ibid.*

[20] *Ibid.*

[21] Statement by former foreign ministers, 'Kosovo Must Be Independent', *International Herald Tribune*, 15 June 2007, http://www.iht.com/bin/print. php?id=6153178.

[22] 'Rossiya Kategoricheski Protiv Navyazyvaniya Belgradu Tesheniy po Kosovo, Kotoryye ne Sootvetstvovali by Serbskim Interesam – Kokoshin', 6 February 2007, http://www.er-duma. ru/news/20695.

[23] 'MID RF: Na Peregovorakh po Kosovo Rossiya Podderzhit Serbov', Newsru.

com, 24 March 2006, http://www.newsru. com/russia/24mar2006/kosovo.html; 'Chernov: Status Abkhazii Dolzhen Opredelyatsya po Analogii s Kosovo', RIA Novosti, 11 April 2007, http://www. rian.ru/politics/20070411/63444021.html.

24 Putin, 'Interview Zhurnalistam Pechatnykh Sredstv Massovoy Informatsii iz Stran-Chlenov "Gruppy Vos'mi"'.

25 Nadejda M. Victor, 'Russia's Gas Crunch', Washington Post, 6 April 2006, http://www. washingtonpost.com/wp-dyn/content/ article/2006/04/05/AR2006040501954. html; Vladimir Milov, 'Ne Sgoret' by Sinim Plamenem', report of seminar presentation to the Higher Economics School, Moscow, 27 September 2006, http://www. hse.ru/temp/2006/09_27_seminar2.shtml.

26 For the Moscow Treaty, see http://www. state.gov/t/ac/trt/18016.htm.

27 Putin, 'Vystupleniya i Diskussiya na Myunkhenskoy Konferentsii po Voprosam Politiki Bezopasnosti'.

28 Kier A. Lieber and Daryl G. Press, 'The Rise of U.S. Nuclear Primacy', Foreign Affairs, March–April 2006, http://www. foreignaffairs.org/20060301faessay85204/ keir-a-lieber-daryl-g-press/the-rise-of-u-s-nuclear-primacy.html?mode=print.

29 Mikhail Leontyev, 'SShA Stremitsya k Strategicheskomu Prevoskhodstvu, a ne Obespecheniyu Bezopasnosti', 29 March 2006, www.kreml.org/interview/ 114148335?mode+print; Aleksey Pushkov, 'Postscriptum', 25 June 2006, http://www. tvc.ru/center/index/id/40101000080444-2006-06-25.html; 'SShA Poluchili Shans Unichtozhit' Rossiyu Odnim Udarom', Lenta.ru, 22 March 2006, http://www. lenta.ru/news/2006/03/22/nuclear/.

30 Sergei Rogov, 'Stavka na Yadernyy Shchit', Nezavisimaya Gazeta, 4 August 2000.

31 See 'Voyennaya Doktrina Rossiyskoy Federatsii' [Russian Military Doctrine], http://www.scrf.gov.ru/documents/33. html; Oleg Falichev, 'Yadernyy Garant Nashey Nezavisimosti', Krasnaya Zvezda, 12 January 2005.

32 See 'Voyennykh Operatsiy NATO na Territorii SNG ne Budet', Rossiskaya Gazeta, 15 September 2001, www.oxpaha. ru/publisher_234_4159.

33 Mikhail Ivanov, 'Will the Taliban Reap the Whirlwind?', Caucasus Reporting Service, Institute for War and Peace Reporting, 26 May 2000, http://iwpr. net/?p=crs&s=f&o=160952&apc_ state=henicrs2000.

34 Sergei Blagov, 'Russia Drops Anchor in Central Asia', Asia Times Online, 25 October 2003, http://www.atimes.com/ atimes/Central_Asia/EJ25Ag01.html.

35 'Declaration of Heads of Member States of Shanghai Cooperation Organisation', Astana, Kazakhstan, 5 July 2005, http://www.sectsco.org/news_detail. asp?id=500&LanguageID=2.

36 Author's personal communication with SCO summit participant.

37 'Last US Plane Leaves Uzbek Base', BBC News, 21 November 2005, http://news. bbc.co.uk/2/hi/asia-pacific/4457844.stm; see also text of treaty between Russia and Uzbekistan, 'Dogovor o Soyuznicheskikh Otnosheniyakh Mezhdu Rossiyskoy Federatsiey i Respublikoy Uzbekistan', http://www.mid.ru/ns-rsng.nsf/ 6bc38aceada6e44b432569e700419ef5/ 432569d800221466c3256eb600317a9f?Ope nDocument.

38 Oleg Yelenskiy, 'Pogranichnikov Vernut', Aviabazu Rashirit: Kyrgizia Otkryvaet Vorota dlya Uvelisheniya Rossiyskogo Voyennogo Prisutstviya v Tsentral'noy Azii', Nezavisimoye Voyennoye Obozreniye, 25 May 2007, http://nvo. ng.ru/printed/7325.

39 See 'Russia Wants Anti-Drug Belt to be Created Around Afghanistan', Interfax, 21 April 2006, http://en.civilg8.ru/1443. php. Also 'NATO: US Ambassador to NATO Discusses Russia, Afghanistan', Radio Free Europe/Radio Liberty, 1 June 2007, http://www.rferl.org/featuresarti-cle/2007/6/EDA20945-5A74-4FEF-B778-287FD164FCE7.html.

40 'Kitayskiy Faktor v Novoy Strukture Mezhdunarodnykh Otnosheniy i Strategiya Rossii', nikitskyclub. ru, 22 September 2004, http://

www.nikitskyclub.ru/article.
php?idpublication=4&idissue=32.

41 Lionel Beehner, 'Russia–Iran Arms
Trade', Backgrounder, Council on
Foreign Relations, 1 November 2006,
http://www.cfr.org/publication/11869/#6;
Richard Grimmet, *Conventional Arms
Transfers to Developing Nations, 1998-2005*
(Washington DC: Congressional Research
Service, 23 October 2006), http://www.
fas.org/sgp/crs/weapons/RL33696.pdf;
Kenneth Katzman, *Iran: Arms and Weapons
of Mass Destruction Suppliers*, (Washington
DC: Congressional Research Service, 3
January 2003), http://www.fas.org/spp/
starwars/crs/RL30551.pdf.

42 See for example interview with Russian
Foreign Minister Sergei Lavrov in
Libre Belgique, posted on the website
of the Russian embassy in Brussels, 22
June 2005, http://www.belgium.mid.
ru/press/024_ru.html.

43 Interview with former State Department
official.

44 'CFE Treaty on Brink of Collapse, Iran
Threat Overblown – Russia Gen.', RIA
Novosti, 10 May 2007, http://en.rian.ru/
russia/20070510/65265934.html.

45 Aleksey Arbatov, *Bezopasnost': Rossiyskiy
Vybor* (Moscow: EPItsentr, 1999), p. 307.

46 Radio Free Europe/Radio Liberty, 'Iran:
Is Russia's Offer Just a Diplomatic
Device?', 13 February 2006, http://
www.rferl.org/featuresarticle/2006/02/
10b0a4f8-5260-4e98-8a90-588f1d75f9ab.
html; David E. Sanger and William J.
Broad, 'Bush and Putin Want Iran to
Treat Uranium in Russia', *New York
Times*, 18 November 2005, http://www.
iranfocus.com/modules/news/article.
php?storyid=4478.

47 'Iran to Be Offered Nuke Compromise',
CNN.com, 10 November 2005,
http://www.cnn.com/2005/WORLD/
meast/11/10/iran.nuclear/index.
html.

48 'Bush, Putin, Agree to Fight Spread of
Nuclear Arms', CNN.com, 24 February
2005, http://www.cnn.com/2005/WORLD/
europe/02/24/bush.europe/index.html.

49 A.D. Bogaturov, 'Vashington ne Sozdaval
Antiiranskuyu Koalitsiyu', *Nezavisimaya
Gazeta*, 13 February 2006.

50 Leonid Radzikhovskiy, 'Imperskiy Gaz',
Vzglyad, 14 December 2005, http://www.
vzglyad.ru/columns/2005/12/14/15623.
html.

51 'UN Passes New Iran Sanctions
Resolution', Radio Free Europe/Radio
Liberty, 24 March 2007, http://www.rferl.
org/featuresarticle/2007/03/E8E280A6-
20DF-435A-B6C5-FAC207A7937F.html;

52 'Iran Unhappy with Slow Construction
of Bushehr NPP', RIA Novosti, 19
February 2007, http://en.rian.ru/
world/20070219/60975701.html; Elaine
Sciolino, David E. Sanger, Helene
Cooper, 'Russia tells Iran it Must Suspend
Uranium Project', *New York Times*, 20
March 2007; Associated Press, 'Russia:
Late Payments May Irresistibly Harm Iran
Nuclear Plant Construction', 14 March
2007, Haaretz.com, http://www.haaretz.
com/hasen/spages/837811.html; Stephen
Blank, 'Russia Reviews the Limits of
Nuclear Cooperation with Iran', Eurasia
Insight, 28 March 2007, http://www.eura-
sianet.org/departments/insight/articles/
eav032807_pr.shtml.

53 See http://www.gnep.energy.gov/gnep
PRs/gnepPR052107.htm; Samuel W.
Bodman, 'Remarks as Prepared for
Secretary Bodman, to Carnegie
Endowment for International Peace,
Moscow Center', 16 March 2006, http://
moscow.usembassy.gov/embassy/
transcript.php?record_id=150.

54 For a rough indication of the kind of sums
likely to be involved, see Peter Baker, 'US
and Russia to Enter Civilian Nuclear Pact',
Washington Post, 8 July 2006, http://www.
washingtonpost.com/wp-dyn/content/
article/2006/07/07/AR2006070701588.
html. It is impossible to say with any
certainty how much the remainder of the
work at Bushehr is worth, but it is likely
to be considerably less than any profits
from this scheme.

55 'U.S./Russia: Former U.S. Ambassador
Assesses Summit', Radio Free Europe/

Radio Liberty, 3 July 2007, http://www.rferl. org/featuresarticle/2007/07/79B9713C-65FE-49FD-909E-0A4849D7DDEE.html; 'Declaration on Nuclear Energy and Nonproliferation: Joint Actions', 3 July 2007, http://www.whitehouse.gov/news/releases/2007/07/20070703.html. For the run-up to the signature of the agreement, see Baker, 'US and Russia to Enter Civilian Nuclear Pact' and Miles A. Pomper, 'Bush, Putin to Seek Nuclear Cooperation Pact', *Arms Control Today*, September 2006, http://www.armscontrol.org/act/2006_09/bushputinpact.asp.

56 For an example of the kinds of sensitivities at play here, see the offence taken by the failure of Russian businessman Aleksei Mordashov to take over Luxembourg steelmaker Arcelor in 2006, which was construed by many in Russia as anti-Russian prejudice. Heather Timmons and Andrew Kramer, 'Some See Russophobia in Arcelor's Decision', *International Herald Tribune*, 27 June 2006, http://www.iht.com/articles/2006/06/27/europe/web.0627russia.php; David Gow and Mark Hollingsworth, 'Mittal Raises Bid to Halt Russian "Cakewalk"', *Guardian*, 24 June 2006, http://business.guardian.co.uk/story/0,,1804834,00.html.

57 See for example 'Kitayskiy Faktor v Novoy Strukture Mezhdunarodnykh Otnosheniy i Strategiya Rossii'.

58 'Strategiya dlya Rossii: Novoye Osvoyeniye Sibiri i Dal'nego Vostoka', Council for Foreign and Defence Policy, 2001, http://www.svop.ru/live/materials.asp?m_id=6752.

59 *Mir Vokrug Rossii: 2017, Kontury Nedalekogo Budushchego*, p. 97.

60 'Putin Razreshil Zhitelyam Severa Sozdavat' Obshchiny', Lenta.ru, 21 July 2000, http://www.lenta.ru/russia/2000/07/21/far_east/_Printed.htm.

61 'Arbatov: Rossiya Stanovitsya Mladshim Voyennym Partnerom Kitaya', *Russia in Global Affairs*, 24 August 2005, http://www.globalaffairs.ru/news/4526.html.

62 'Russia's Far East Population Continues to Dwindle', *Vladivostok News*, 15 March 2007, http://vn.vladnews.ru/issue560/Special_reports/Russias_Far_East_population_continues_to_dwindle?PHPSESSID=hmta2hpnbgi9lst6d7saik3n87.

63 Natalya Alyakinskaya, 'Labor Shortage Puts Russian Economy at Risk', *Moscow News*, 19 June 2007, http://english.mn.ru/english/issue.php?2007-9-9.

64 Blagov, 'Moscow Appears to Waver over Pacific Pipeline Route', *Eurasia Daily Monitor*, Jamestown Foundation, 13 April 2005, http://www.jamestown.org/edm/article.php?article_id=2369591; Energy Information Administration, US Department of Energy, 'Country Analysis Briefs: Russia', April 2007, http://www.eia.doe.gov/emeu/cabs/Russia/Full.html.

65 Kramer, 'Putin Threatens to Send Energy Exports East', *International Herald Tribune*, 27 April 2006, http://www.iht.com/articles/2006/04/26/news/russia.php.

66 Sergei Ivanov, 'V Tselom My, Konechno, Yevropeytsy, a Ne Aziaty', interview in *Financial Times*, 24 April 2007, reprinted in Polit.ru, http://polit.ru/dossie/2007/04/26/ivanov_print.html.

Chapter Three

1 Neil Buckley, 'Russia Steps up "Ethnic Cleansing" of Georgians', *Financial Times*, 7 October 2006, http://www.ft.com/cms/s/8d65f612-559f-11db-acba-0000779e2340.html; Masha Lipman, '"Enemy" Schoolchildren in Moscow', *Washington Post*, 21 October 2006, http://www.washingtonpost.com/wp-dyn/content/article/2006/10/20/AR2006102001362.html.

2 Levada Centre, 'Konflikt s Gruziyey: Mnieniya i Otsenki Rossiyan', 20

October 2006, http://www.levada.ru/press/2006102003.print.html. The Levada Centre is a leading independent Russian polling organisation.

3 Levada Centre, 'Rossiyane o Sobytiyakh na Ukraine', 28 February 2005, http://www.levada.ru/press/2005022801.print.html.

4 L. Sedov, 'Strana i Mir', Levada Centre, 6 May 2006, http://www.levada.ru/press/2006050600.print.html.

5 'Obraz Vraga', *Ekspert* Online, 1 June 2007, http://www.expert.ru/news/2007/06/01/eesti/.

6 See http://www.inosmi.ru/; http://www.inopressa.ru/.

7 Levada Centre, 'Uroven' Osnashchennosti Telefonnoy Svyaz'yu i Internetom', 5 October 2006, http://www.levada.ru/press/2006100502.print.html.

8 'Yandex Issledoval Russkoyazychnuyu Blogospheru', 26 September 2006, http://company.yandex.ru/news/2006/0926/index.xml.

9 Putin, 'Poslaniye Federal'nomu Sobraniyu Rossiyskoy Federatsii', 25 April 2005, http://www.kremlin.ru/appears/2005/04/25/1223_type63372type63374type82634_87049.shtml.

10 Levada Centre, 'Rossiyane o Raspade SSSR i Perspektivakh SNG', http://www.levada.ru/press/2006120701.print.html.

11 Levada Centre, 'Itogi "Perestroyki": 20 Let Spustya', 11 March 2005, http://www.levada.ru/press/2005031100.print.html.

12 Interfax, 'Most Russians Back Higher Gas Prices for Ukraine', 27 December 2005, reported in Johnson's Russia List, JRL 9328, http://www.cdi.org/russia/johnson/9328-18.cfm.

13 Levada Centre, 'Chto Prinesla Rossii Epokha B.N. Yeltsina?', 30 January 2006, http://www.levada.ru/.

14 See 'Russian President Vladimir Putin Signs New NGO Law', International Center for Not-for-Profit Law, 19 January 2006, http://www.icnl.org/knowledge/news/2006/01-19.htm.

15 See for instance 'UK Diplomats in Moscow Spying Row', BBC News, 23 January 2006, http://news.bbc.co.uk/1/hi/world/europe/4638136.stm

16 Levada Centre, 'Sotsial'no-politicheskaya Situatsiya v Strane v Octyabre 2006 goda', http://www.levada.ru/press/2006110202.print.html.

17 Aleksey Aronov, 'Chto Derzhit na Plavu Kapitanov Rossiyskogo Biznesa', 26 June 2007, *Finansovuy Izvestiya*, http://www.finiz.ru/cfin/tmpl-art/id_art-1236836.

18 For these and other figures, see *ibid.* and Levada Centre, 'Sotsial'no-politicheskaya Situatsiya v Strane v Avguste 2006 goda', http://www.levada.ru/press/2006091302.print.html; 'Sotsial'no-Politicheskaya Situatsiya v Strane v Sentyabre 2006 goda', http://www.levada.ru/press/2006100301.print.html.

19 'Abonentov Sotovoy Svyazi v RF Stalo Bol'she Chem Zhiteley', *Nezavisimaya Gazeta*, 18 June 2006, http://www.ng.ru/economics/2007-06-18/4_cell.html.

20 'Vladislav Surkov Divides Democracy', *Kommersant*, 29 June 2006, http://www.kommersant.com/page.asp?idr=1&id=686274; 'Vladislav Surkov Ob"yasnil Chto Takoye 'Suverennaya Demokratiya', Polit.ru, 20 June 2007, http://www.polit.ru/news/2007/06/20/surkov.popup.html.

21 Putin, 'Zayavleniye dlya Pressy i Otvety na Voprosy v Khode Sovmestnoy Press-Konferentsii s Federal'nym Avstriyskim Kantslerom Khaiyntsem Fisherom', 23 May 2007, http://www.kremlin.ru.

22 Putin, 'Poslaniye Federal'nomu Sobraniyu Rossiyskoy Federatsii', 26 April 2007, http://www.kremlin.ru.

23 Program on International Policy Attitudes, 'Russians Support Putin's Re-nationalization of Oil, Control of Media, But See Democratic Future', http://www.worldpublicopinion.org/incl/printable_version.php?pnt=224.

24 Levada Centre, 'Oppozitsionnye Protesty', 29 March 2007, http://www.levada.ru/press/2007032902.print.html.

25 *Ibid.*

26 These had previously been paid in kind; in free transport, medicines etc. Concerns

about the devaluing effects of inflation and inadequate compensation were behind the protests. See Charles Gurin, 'Russia Hit by A Wave of Protests Against Government Benefits Policy', *Eurasian Daily Monitor*, Jamestown Foundation, 14 January 2005, http://www.jamestown. org/edm/article.php?article_id=2369094.

27 Claire Bigg, 'Russia: Kondopoga Violence Continues Unabated', Radio Free Europe/ Radio Liberty, 6 September 2006, http:// www.rferl.org/featuresarticle/2006/09/ 6cc8626f-be02-4054-957b-d0872dc41157. html.

28 Lipman, 'Russia's Apolitical Middle', *Washington Post*, 4 June 2007, http://www. washingtonpost.com/wp-dyn/content/ article/2007/06/03/AR2007060300950. html.

29 Mark Franchetti, 'West feels Icy Blast of Russian Nationalism', *Sunday Times*, 16 July 2006, http://www.timesonline.co.uk/ tol/news/world/article688358.ece; Yury

Filippov, 'Nationalism Threatens Russia', RIA Novosti, 5 April 2006, http://en.rian. ru/analysis/20060405/45233440.html.

30 Jeff Mankoff, 'Kremlin Turns a Blind Eye to Racism', *International Herald Tribune*, 20 August 2007, http://www.iht.com/articles/ 2007/08/20/opinion/edmankoff.php.

31 *Ibid*.

32 A situation that some Kremlin officials and associates have been known to justify privately in terms of defending the country from the nationalists and other radicals that Putin's critics tend to fear.

33 Reasons behind the ideology/party vacuum in modern-day Russia are summarised by Stephen E. Hanson, 'Ideology and Party System Development', paper prepared for the annual meeting of the American Political Science Association, 1 August–4 September 2006, http:// sitemaker.umich.edu/comparative. speaker.series/files/stephen_hanson.pdf.

Chapter Four

1 *CIA World Factbook*, https://www.cia. gov/library/publications/the-world-factbook/geos/rs.html#Econ; Buckley, 'Russia's Debt Default is History', *Financial Times*, 24 April 2007, http:// www.ft.com/cms/s/6ad9ce08-f27e-11db-a454-000b5df10621.html; World Bank, 'Russian Economic Report', no. 14, June 2007, http://siteresources.worldbank.org/ INTRUSSIANFEDERATION/Resources/ RER14_eng_full.pdf; United Nations Conference on Trade and Development press release, 'Foreign Direct Investment Rose by 34% in 2006', 9 January 2007, http://www.unctad.org/Templates/ Webflyer.asp?docID=7993&intItemID=15 28&lang=1.

2 Buckley, 'Russia's Debt Default is History'.

3 Interview with Ivanov, 'Triada Natsional'nykh Tsennostey', *Izvestiya*,

13 July 2006, http://www.izvestia. ru/politic/article3094592/?print.

4 'Stenograficheskiy Otchyot o Zasedanii XI Peterburgskogo Mezhdunarodnogo Ekonomicheskogo Foruma po Teme "Konkurentnosposobnaya Yevraziya – Prostranstvo Doveriya"'.

5 See interview with Ivanov, 'Triada Natsional'nykh Tsennostey'.

6 Information on Russia's economic performance is available from multiple sources, including the World Bank, http://web.worldbank.org/WBSITE/ EXTERNAL/COUNTRIES/ECAEXT/ RUSSIANFEDERATIONEXTN/0,,menuP K:305605~pagePK:141159~piPK:141110~th eSitePK:305600,00.html, and the *CIA World Factbook*, which provides a useful overview of Russia, including of its economy https://www.cia.gov/library/publications/ the-world-factbook/geos/rs.html.

7   See Celeste A. Wallander, 'Russian Foreign Policy: The Implications of Pragmatism for U.S. Policy', testimony before the House Committee on International Relations, Subcommittee on Europe, 27 February 2002, http://www.csis.org/media/csis/congress/ts020227wallender.pdf.

8   See 'Beginning of the Meeting on Developing Nanotechnology', report of Kremlin planning meeting, 18 April 2007, http://www.kremlin.ru.

9   Levada Centre, 'Osenneye Nastroyeniye Rossiyan', 11 October 2006, http://www.levada.ru/press/2006101105.html.

10   Natalia Cherviakova, 'Russia on the Edge of Demographic Catastrophe', Pravda.ru, 11 November 2003, http://english.pravda.ru/science/health/11-11-2003/4050-population-0; Nicholas Eberstadt, 'Russia, the Sick Man of Europe', *The Public Interest*, Winter 2005, http://findarticles.com/p/articles/mi_m0377/is_158/ai_n8680968/print.

11   'Russian Population in Steep Decline', BBC News, 24 October 2000, http://news.bbc.co.uk/1/hi/world/europe/988723.stm.

12   'Demograficheskaya Strashilka', *Ekspert*, 5 March 2007, http://www.expert.ru/printissues/xpert/2007/09/demograficheskaya_strashilka.

13   World Bank, 'Report: Labor Migration Likely to Grow in Europe and Central Asia', 16 January 2007, http://web.worldbank.org/WBSITE/EXTERNAL/TOPICS/EXTPOVERTY/ 0,,contentMDK:21183561~pagePK:148956~piPK:216618~theSitePK:336992,00.html.

14   'Defitsit Rabochey Sily: Russkiy Krest-2?', *Demoskop Weekly*, Tsentr Demografii i Ekologii Cheloveka [Institute of National Economic Forecasting of the Russian Academy of Sciences], http://www.polit.ru/research/2007/03/09/demoscope277_print.html.

15   Yelena Yarikov, 'Nekomu Stroit' i Programmirovat', *Vedomosti*, 24 May 2007, http://www.vedomosti.ru/newspaper/article.shtml?2007/05/24/126348 [article available by subscription only].

16   *CIA World Factbook*, https://www.cia.gov/library/publications/the-world-factbook/print/rs.html; International Database, US Census Bureau, http://www.infoplease.com/ipa/A0004393.html.

17   Eberstadt, 'Population/Health/Ageing: The Achilles Heel in Russian Economic Development', presentation to the Center for Strategic and International Studies, Washington DC, 22 July 2005, http://www.csis.org/media/csis/events/050722_eberstadt_presentation.pdf.

18   National Intelligence Council, 'The Next Wave of HIV/AIDS: Nigeria, Ethiopia, Russia, India, and China', September 2002, http://www.fas.org/irp/nic/hiv-aids.html.

19   'Putin Highlights Ageing Population, Alcoholism, Offers Solutions', RIA Novosti, 21 December 2006, http://en.rian.ru/russia/20061221/57507732.html.

20   Nadezhda Ivanitskaya, Maksim Glinkin and Boris Grozovskiy, 'Fantasticheskaya Demografiya', *Vedomosti*, 23 May 2007, http://www.vedomosti.ru/newspaper/print.shtml?2007/05/23/126276 [article available by subscription only].

21   United Nations Development Programme, 'Russia's Regions: Facts and Figures', http://www.undp.ru/index.phtml?iso+RU&lid=1&cmd=text&id=187.

22   World Bank, 'Russian Economic Report', no. 14, June 2007; see also Mikhail Sergeyev, 'Vsemirnyy Bank Raskritikoval Ekonomiku Rossii', *Nezavisimaya Gazeta*, 7 June 2007, http://ng.ru/printed/78945.

23   UN Development Programme, 'Russia's Regions: Facts and Figures'.

24   Sergeyev, 'Vsemirnyy Bank Raskritikoval Ekonomiku Rossii', World Bank, 'Russian Economic Report', no. 14.

25   In 2002, there were approximately 756,000km of paved roads; in 2005, only 706,000km.

26   Vladimir Milov, 'Globalist: Avtodorozhnyye Itogi', *Vedomosti*, 16 May 2007, http://www.vedomosti.ru/newspaper.print.shtml?2007/05/16/125846 [article available subscription only].

27   http://www.transparency.org/policy_research/surveys_indices/cpi/2006 .

28 International Property Rights Index, 2007 Report, http://www.internationalpropertyrightsindex.org/UserFiles/File/PRA_Interior_LowRes.pdf; see also Anna Smolchenko, 'Russia Ranks 63rd in Property Rights Poll', *Moscow Times*, 7 March 2007.

29 World Bank, 'Russian Economic Report', no. 14.

30 For comparison, US arms exports in 2006 were $11.5 billion.

31 Victor Litovkin, 'Russian Arms Exports Break Records', Spacewar.com, 8 March 2007, http://www.spacewar.com/reports/Russian_Arms_Exports_Break_Records_999.html.

32 '80% of Russia's Defense Industry Is Obsolete', Rosbalt, 18 August 2004, http://www.cdi.org/russia/270-14.cfm; 'Russia Spends $1.1bn Annually on Defense Industry – Gov't', RIA Novosti, 15 March 2007; Blank, 'Rosoboroneksport: Arms Sales and the Structure of Russian Defense Industry', US Army Strategic Studies Institute, January 2007, http://www.strategicstudiesinstitute.army.mil/pdffiles/PUB749.pdf.

33 Eugene Kogan, 'Russia–China Aerospace Industries: From Cooperation to Disengagement', *China Brief*, vol. 4, no. 19, 30 September 2004, http://www.jamestown.org/china_brief/article.php?articleid=2372918&printthis=1; Aleksandra Gritskova, Konstantin Lantratov and Gennady Sysoev, 'China Lays Down Russian Arms', *Kommersant*, 7 May 2007, http://www.kommersant.com/p763776/r_529/military-technical_cooperation_China/.

34 Aleksandr Golts, 'Russia's Arms Exports', *Special Operations Technology*, 24 February 2005, http://www.special-operations-technology.com/print_article.cfm?DocID=891.

35 'Russia Spends $1.1bn Annually on Defense Industry – Gov't'.

36 Nikolai Kirillov, 'Akhillesova Pyata Oboronospsobnosti Strany', *Nezavisimoye Voyennoye Obozreniye*, 10 November 2006, http://nvo.ng.ru/armament/2006-11-10/6_opk.html; Viktor Myasnikov, 'Voyennaya Promyshlennost' Spolzla za Gran'

Bankrotstva', *Nezavisimoye Voyennoye Obozreniye*, 28 April 2006, http://nvo.ng.ru/wars/2006-04-28/1_industry.html.

37 Kirillov, 'Akhillesova Pyata Oboronospsobnosti Strany'.

38 Ali Aliyev, 'Eshchyo Odin Rossiyskiy Chebol', *Ekspert* Online, 20 June 2007, http://www.expert.ru/articles/2007/06/20/rostehnologii/print.

39 Statistics derived from 'Country Briefings: Russia', Economist.com, on 30 May 2007.

40 Information from 'Country Briefings: Russia: Economic Structure', Economist.com, as at 30 May 2007, http://www.economist.co.uk/countries/Russia/profile.cfm?folder=Profile-Economic%20Structure.

41 European Commission, 'Bilateral Trade Relations: Russia', http://ec.europa.eu/trade/issues/bilateral/countries/russia/index_en.htm.

42 Judy Dempsey, 'Problem for Europe: Russia Needs Gas, Too', *International Herald Tribune*, 21 November 2006, http://www.iht.com/articles/2006/11/21/news/energy.php.

43 Dov Lynch, 'Russia's Strategic Partnership with Europe', *The Washington Quarterly*, vol. 27, no. 2, Spring 2004, http://www.twq.com/04spring/docs/04spring_lynch.pdf.

44 Readers may note that the figures quoted in the breakdown of the quantities of gas needed slightly exceed the figure for total demand; the figures are as they appear in the source (see below), and are approximations only.

45 Sergei Dubinin, 'Epokha Defitistov', Gazeta.ru, 19 June 2007, http://www.gazeta.ru/comments/2007/06/19_a_1823690.shtml?print.

46 *Ibid.*

47 For example, the underwater Shtokman field in the Barents Sea is estimated to cost some $20bn to develop; the cost of further developing Gazprom's fields in the Yamal Peninsula is as high as $50–80bn. Victor, 'Russian Geopolitical Geometry Through a Gas Prism', briefing to the Center for Strategic and International Studies, Washington DC, 9 May 2006.

48 Judy Clark and Nina Rach, 'Gazprom to Develop Shtokman Alone, Pipe Gas to Europe', *Oil and Gas Journal*, 10 October 2006, http://www.energybulletin.net/21287.html.

49 Miriam Elder, 'Total to Get Reserves Under Shtokman Deal', *Moscow Times*, 16 July 2007.

50 'Stenograficheskiy Otchyot o Zasedanii XI Peterburgskogo Mezhdunarodnogo Ekonomicheskogo Foruma po Teme "Konkurentnosposobnaya Yevraziya – Prostranstvo Doveriya"'.

51 *Ibid.*

52 See Timmons and Kramer, 'Some See Russophobia in Arcelor's Decision'.

Chapter Five

1 There are signs from time to time that some senior military officers feel marginalised in Putin's national security apparatus. For example, Leonid Ivashov, a retired general known for his conservative views, commented on the appointment of Anatoly Serdyukov, a former tax official and furniture salesman, as Russia's newest defence minister in February 2007 that 'It was a spit in the face that is why the generals were sitting and wiping [it]. It is a humiliation of the army, humiliation of the man with epaulettes … [I am receiving] many phone calls from the troops, from the general staff … [some even say] that it's good that [he] appointed a man, because Putin could have appointed his labrador'. 'Razvorot' radio programme, Ekho Moskvy radio station, Moscow, 16 February 2007, http://www.echo.msk.ru/programs/razvorot/49683/index.phtml.

2 See US Defense Intelligence Agency, 'Chapter II, 1983: Strategic Forces' in the series 'Soviet Military Power, 1983–1991', http://www.fas.org/irp/dia/product/smp_83_ch2.htm. Clearly, the Soviet and Russian militaries are very different beasts, their divergent qualities too many to be discussed here (indeed the differences between them are possibly too stark to allow for meaningful comparison), nevertheless, the dramatic contrast between the state of the two militaries in the periods mentioned is striking.

3 See Anatol Lieven, *Chechnya: Tombstone of Russian Power* (New Haven and London: Yale University Press, 1998).

4 William E. Odom, *The Collapse of the Soviet Military* (New Haven and London: Yale University Press, 2000); Eugene B. Rumer, *The End of a Monolith: The Politics of Military Reform in the Soviet Armed Forces* (Santa Monica: RAND, 1991).

5 'Russia Revises Military Doctrine to Reflect Global Changes', Spacewar.com, 6 March 2007, http://www.spacewar.com/reports/Russia_Revises_Military_Doctrine_To_Reflect_Global_Changes_999.html.

6 Julian Cooper, Centre for Russian and East European Studies, University of Birmingham, 'Military Expenditure in the 2005 and 2006 Federal Budgets of the Russian Federation', research note, January 2006, http://www.sipri.org/contents/milap/cooper_russia_20060130.

7 IISS, *The Military Balance 2006* (Abingdon: Routledge for the IISS, 2006).

8 The numbers of servicemen are taken from IISS, *The Military Balance 2006*. A breakdown of the services and branches of the Russian military can be found at Ministerstvo Oborony Rossiyskoy Federatsii [Russian defence ministry], 'Struktura Vooruzhennykh Sil', http://www.mil.ru/848/1045/index.shtml.

9 Since the fall of the Soviet Union, there has been a proliferation of armed, uniformed services that do not report to the ministry of defence. Armed and uniformed men

serve as ministry of the interior troops, ministry of emergencies troops and border guards, and in the Federal Guard Service, the tax police and various other agencies.

10   Information derived from RussianForces. org, website of independent arms control and nuclear information project 'Russian Nuclear Forces Project', http://russian-forces.org/current/.

11   Lieber and Press, 'The Rise of U.S. Nuclear Primacy'.

12   Podvig, 'Speaking of Nuclear Primacy', RussianForces.org, 10 March 2006, http://russianforces.org/blog/2006/03/speaking_of_nuclear_primacy.shtml.

13   Aleksey Nikolsky, 'Mutatsiya "Topolya"', *Vedomosti*, 5 May 2007, http://www.vedomosti.ru/newspaper/article.shtml?2007/05/08/125470.

14   *Ibid.*

15   *Ibid.*

16   *Ibid.*

17   RussianForces.org, http://russianforces.org/navy/.

18   *Ibid.*

19   *Ibid.*

20   *Ibid.*

21   Viktor Litovkin, '"Dolgorukogo" Vyveli v Shampanskoye', *Nezavisimoye Voyennoye Obozreniye*, 20 April 2007, http://nvo.ng.ru/printed/7280.

22   Vladimir Gundarev, 'Poslednyaya "Ustalaya Podlodka"', *Nezavisimoye Voyennoye Obozreniye*, 8 June 2007, http://nvo.ng.ru/printed/7356.

23   *Ibid.*

24   Pavel Felgenhauer, 'Degradation of the Russian Military: General Anatoli Kvashnin', *Perspective*, vol 15, no. 1, October–November 2004, http://www.bu.edu/iscip/vol15/Felgenhauer.html.

25   Roger McDermott, 'Russian Military Reform: Reduction and Restructuring, Again', *Eurasia Daily Monitor*, vol. 1, no. 110, 21 October 2004, http://www.jamestown.org/publications_details.php?volume_id=401&issue_id=3115&article_id=2368729; 'Russia Plans Wide Military Reform', BBC News,

24 May 2006, http://news.bbc.co.uk/1/hi/world/europe/5013936.stm.

26   Vadim Solovyov, 'Voyennaya Reforma Ob'yavlena Bessrochnoy', *Nezavisimoye Voyennoye Obozreniye*, 26 January 2007, http://nvo.ng.ru/wars/2007-01-26/1_reforma.html.

27   Keir Giles, 'Where Have All the Soldiers Gone?: Russia's Military Plans Versus Demographic Reality', Conflict Studies Research Centre, Defence Academy of the United Kingdom, Russian Series, 06/47, October 2006. Accessible from http://www.defac.ac.uk/colleges/csrc/document-listings/caucasus-publications.

28   Giles, 'Military Service in Russia: No New Model Army', Conflict Studies Research Centre, Russian Series, 07/18, May 2007, accessible from http://www.defac.ac.uk/colleges/csrc/document-listings/russian/; Felgenhauer, 'Russian Military: After Ivanov', Institute for the Study of Conflict, Ideology, and Policy, 21 May 2007, http://www.bu.edu/phpbin/news-cms/news/?dept=732&id=45147; Anatoly Tsyganok, 'Budet li v Rossiyskoy Armii Professional'nyy Serzhant?', Polit. ru, 4 June 2007, http://www.polit.ru/author/2007/05/30/serzhant.html

29   Tsyganok, 'Razgovory o Perevooruzhenii Rossiyskoy Armii – Mif', 30 June 2006, 'Independent Expert Opinion' (weblog), www.tsiganok.ru/; 'Gosoboronoilluziya Podmenila Gosoboronpokaz', www.tsiganok.ru.

30   Andrey Frolov, 'Russian Defense Procurement in 2007', *Moscow Defense Brief*, no. 8, http://www.mdb.cast.ru/mdb/2-2007/item1/item2/.

31   *Ibid.*

32   Kirillov, 'Akhillesova Pyata Oboronosposobnosti Strany'; Myasnikov, 'Voyenprom Yeshchyo Likhoradit', *Nezavisimoye Voyennoye Obozreniye*, 23 December 2005; Igor Plugataryov, 'Novyye "Mi" i "Ka" Letyat v Proshloye', *Nezavisimoye Voyennoye Obozreniye*, 25 May 2007, http://nvo.ng.ru/printed/7332; Mikhail Lukanin, 'Oboronka Zadirayet Tseny', *Nezavisimoye Voyennoye Obozreniye*,

6 April 2007, http://nvo.ng.ru/printed/7251; Aleksandr Karpovich and Oleg Bulatov, '"Bereg" Blizhnego Deystviya', *Nezavisimoye Voyennoye Obozreniye*, 8 June 2007, http://nvo.ng.ru/printed/7359.

33 'Aktual'nyye Zadachi Razvitiya Vooruzhennykh sil Rossiyskoy Federatsii', Russian defence ministry publication, 2003.

34 See note 9.

Conclusion

1 Trenin, 'Reading Russia Right', Policy Brief No. 42, Carnegie Endowment for International Peace, October 2005, http://www.carnegieendowment.org/files/pb42.trenin.FINAL.pdf.

2 George F. Kennan, 'America and the Russian Future', *Foreign Affairs*, April 1951. The same point was stressed in a Trilateral Commission study published in 2006: Roderic Lyne, Strobe Talbott, Koji Watanabe, 'Engaging with Russia: The Next Phase', *The Triangle Papers*, no. 59 (Washington DC, Paris, Tokyo: The Trilateral Commission, 2006), http://www.trilateral.org/library/stacks/Engaging_With_Russia.pdf.